Mgjlr

A PLACE IN THE CHOIR

FINDING HARMONY IN A WORLD OF MANY VOICES

JOHN JACOBSON

FOREWORD BY MARIAN WRIGHT EDELMAN

ISBN-13: 978-1-42340-842-0
ISBN-10: 1-42340-842-X

Published by Hal Leonard Corporation
7777 W. Bluemound Road
P.O. Box 13819
Milwaukee, WI 53213

Library of Congress Cataloging-in-Publication Data

Jacobson, John.
  A place in the choir : finding harmony in a world of many voices / by John Jacobson ; edited by Sharon Stosur ; foreword by Marian Wright Edelman.
     p. cm.
  Includes index.
  ISBN-13: 978-1-4234-0842-0 (hard cover)
  ISBN-10: 1-4234-0842-X (hardcover)
  1. Jacobson, John. 2. Music teachers—United States—Biography. 3. Music—Instruction and study—United States—Anecdotes. I. Stosur, Sharon. II. Title.
ML423.J116A3 2006
780.71'073—dc22
                                        2006010865

Printed in the U.S.A.

First Edition

Visit Hal Leonard Online at
www.halleonard.com

TO MOTHER

FOREWORD

by Marian Wright Edelman
President and Founder, Children's Defense Fund

The Children's Defense Fund's logo, illustrated by 7-year-old Maria Coté, is a drawing of a bright sun shining on a small boat with a tiny sail adrift on a very wide sea. Above the drawing, in Maria's handwriting, is the ancient traditional fisherman's prayer: "Dear Lord, be good to me. The sea is so wide and my boat is so small."

John Jacobson and Mac Huff used this image in "The Sea Is So Wide," a song they wrote and dedicated to the Children's Defense Fund whose lyrics are included in *A Place in the Choir*:

> *...The sea is so wide, my boat is so small.*
> *Dear Lord, I stand amazed at the wonder of it all.*
> *Adrift on a rolling sea with no guiding star in sight*
> *I feel so alone in the darkness of the night.*
>
> *What I need is your hand. Will you walk by my side?*
> *And see me as I am, my arms are open wide.*
> *We can hope and we can dream for the dawning of a brighter day.*
> *Dear Lord, be good to me and help me find my way, I pray ...*

Far too many of our children could sing these words today. When children and teenagers feel adrift or confused as they try to navigate through life and find their place in the world, they need adults to be ready to take their hands and walk by their side. How many of us have committed to taking our children into our arms and protecting them while we work for a brighter day for all children? How can we make sure every child has help finding his or her way? John Jacobson has it exactly right when he tells us the first thing we must do is remember one key promise: "All God's children got a place in the choir."

I love this simple, profound message. For the dedicated music teachers whose stories are throughout this book, it's a very real motto. You'll meet them taking shy children, "rascally" children, boys who need extra pillows to keep up their Santa suits, girls whose tutus are too tight, and children who just don't seem to fit in anywhere else during the rest of the day—and giving every one of them their special role to play. These teachers have it exactly right when they understand that every child has a song in his or her heart, and when they never give up on helping each one to hear it and learn to sing or play it loud. Those of us who are not music teachers could learn our own lessons from peeking into their classroom doors.

After all, as this book reminds us, in a music class, every child matters. There's the story of the young man whose choir class keeps him coming to school, because he would never be missed in math or English—but if he were absent from the baritone section, people would notice his music was missing. How many other children are slipping through our fingers because no one is there to notice their song? And music is also a true equalizer. It doesn't make a difference whether children are rich or poor, Black or White, what kind of clothes they wear, or what they look like. How many other places will children find this is true?

John Jacobson and musicians like him are 'child advocates' in every sense of the word. They are creating a world where every child is celebrated, every child belongs, every child's gifts are nurtured, and every child feels needed, loved, and *heard*. But that world shouldn't be limited to a music stage. It's the model for the world we should all be striving to create for every child. That's why *A Place in the Choir* is ultimately not a book for musicians or teachers, as much as it celebrates them both. It's a book for anyone who has the chance to change a child's world, and this means it's a book for all of us. We have pushed so many of our children into the tumultuous sea of life in leaky boats without survival gear. It is time now to give all our children the anchor of faith, the rudder of hope, the sails of education, and the paddles of family to keep them going when life's sea gets rough.

All God's children got a place in the choir. Musicians have already learned this lesson. When will the rest of us learn it too? When we become a nation and world that *truly* make a place in their choir for every child, just imagine the song we'll all hear.

TABLE OF CONTENTS

IV. HEROES AND SAINTS

PREFACE

Mostly I like to write little kid songs. Just stuff that rhymes, that makes children giggle and adults tear up. Mostly, that's what I like to do. It has been my privilege to spend the last quarter of a century, (seems like a third) traveling the world teaching children and their teachers songs I like to make up, and sometimes the games or dances that go along with them. It's what I do, still.

My first professional job as a "sort-of" educational-choreographer was at Hueytown High School in the suburbs of Birmingham, Alabama in 1979. White children danced with white children and black children danced with black children. I was naïve and not even a very good choreographer. Things have changed in Hueytown and elsewhere. Me too. Thank goodness. I'm still not the world's greatest choreographer, but I am not naïve; at least not so much so. After Hueytown I was fortunate enough to work in music class-rooms from Fairbanks to Key West, Maine to California. Once I taught a song from Roger Miller's musical *Big River* to a topless choir in Papua, New Guinea. (Not the kind of topless you get here at home!) I taught a Conga dance to about three hundred children in the red mud of Madagascar. In Japan I taught music in an all girls school led by an eighty-year-old nun named Sister Nishikawa. In Germany I led choirs of students from Moldova, Poland, Ukraine, Iceland, the Netherlands, Russia, Slovenia, the Czech Republic, Hungary, and more. I've done teacher workshops for music teachers in seemingly every burg in America, not to mention Canada, the Philippines, Vietnam, Bermuda, France, England, and many other lands where children sing and adults teach them.

Here is what I've learned. "All God's children got a place in the choir." I have borne witness to the fact that in the choir it doesn't matter if you are big or little, tall or short, quick or slow, funny or dull! It does not matter if you are black or white, brown or red, pink, purple, yellow, or covered with rainbow colored polka dots! It does not matter if you are Christian, Jew, Muslim, Buddhist, Shinto, Hindu, or a loud-mouthed Lutheran from Lithuania! It does not matter if you are gay, straight, both, or in love with a Chimpanzee! It does not matter if you are a Democrat, Republican, Socialist, Communist or even a tenor! It does not matter if you wear $150 fashion blue jeans or run around in an ill-tailored gunnysack; if you have blond hair, black hair, no hair, or a head like a Chia pet! It does not matter if you have clear skin, an occasional blemish, or a face full of zits and uncontrollable flaking! What I have learned is as this is true in choir; it is also true in life. We need all of this. It is our blessing.

Perhaps I should say at the outset that if you don't buy this last paragraph you should quit reading this book right now. It will only frustrate you, for this is my mantra. It is my prayer as well as my absolute belief. Every word I utter from here on out is predicated on this highfalutin' premise.

The following chapters are mostly a collection of articles I have written over the past few years, published in *John Jacobson's Music Express*, a magazine published by Hal Leonard Corporation for which I serve as Senior Contributing Writer and Editorial Consultant. What this means is I am the chief collaborator. I can hardly do anything alone! I don't want to. I've included some lyrics of songs that friends and I have written because I like them. Put in your own melody if you so choose. Like my friend Roger says, "Hey, there are only twelve notes. You're always a half step from something that works!"

Sir Elton John and I don't agree on everything, well, he never actually asked for my opinion, but I do agree with him when he sings:

> *And it's all so much bigger than it seems*
> *And it all overwhelms us now and then*
> *And I'm banking on a chance that we believe*
> *That good can still control the hearts of men*

My personal and professional collaborations have been some of the most rewarding experiences of my life, and the line between the two is essentially non-existent. I have had the privilege of working with some of the finest musicians, composers, writers, teachers, and friends who have ever lived. People like Mac Huff, whom I have worked alongside of since we were kids, Roger Emerson who calls me every morning and sings over the phone to brighten my day, Emily Crocker who makes me feel like I can really do stuff, John Higgins who can make anything sound good and, believe me, I've given him some sow's ears to work with over the years,

Moses Hogan my friend and collaborator who used to introduce me by saying we were brothers separated by birth and Mom simply left him out in the sun a little longer. Alan Billingsley, Rollo Dilworth, Kirby Shaw, Cristi Cary Miller, Myra Murray, Janet Day, Michael Spresser, Andy Waterman, Chris Koszuta, Tom Anderson, Cheryl and Paul Lavender, and many, many more. Especially Michael Mertens. Sir Elton suggests:

This life's a long old road.
We shouldn't have to walk alone.
But if you find the right companion
You won't feel so worn out when you've grown.
Answer In The Sky

I feel so young.

Throughout this book I will share with you the results of some of our collaborations, and thank my friends for what they have brought to my life and the lives of "children" in the choir. By the way, I will wager all that I am, that each and every one of them believes; "All God's children got a place in the choir."

I like run-on sentences and "cheese-y" jokes. You see I grew up in Wisconsin, where to be "cheese-y" is a grand compliment. I like sentimentality. Okay, sap. I love teachers, especially music teachers, and so to them and to my mother, I dedicate this collection. I am so very proud to be your peer.

And lastly I give my heart to children. Children of all shapes and sizes, even grown-up ones like some of you, who feel as though they have never quite found a proper place in this world. It is not true. There's a part waiting for you. The choir that is humankind needs no audition. Do not be afraid. There is a place for you. Sing out!

THE WHITE HOUSE

WASHINGTON

May 25, 1989

Dear Mr. Jacobson:

Barbara and I just wanted to take this opportunity to
express our admiration for your "America Sings!" project.

To have thousands of young people gathered on the Mall,
singing their hearts out in behalf of homeless children
was an inspiration. You not only helped to create a day
of musical beauty and delight but also provided support
for the cause of aiding the needy. Our hope is that
the enthusiasm you've ignited in these young people
will continue to burn bright, inspiring them in further
selfless efforts.

Projects like this never come easy, to say the least.
You deserve tremendous credit for tirelessly working
to make your dream a reality we all can be proud of.
Thank you and God bless you.

Sincerely,

George Bush

Mr. John C. Jacobson
America Sings!, Inc.
Post Office Box 34101
Bethesda, Maryland 20817

CELEBRATE MUSIC

CELEBRATE MUSIC!

When Ida Thompson was still in the womb her mother started the lullabies and nursery songs that she would sing throughout Ida's infancy. Ida would remember "Hush Little Baby Don't You Cry," "Lullaby and Goodnight" and "All the Pretty Little Horses" for every one of the eighty-three years that she walked this planet. The day she was born her granddad played his Hardanger fiddle as Grandmother clapped along, not to the birth but to the music. The celebration of life had begun. From that day forward, every important or even seemingly insignificant moment of Ida's life was accompanied, and often led, by music.

"Pony girl! Pony girl! Won't you be my pony girl?" It was Grandpa again with his trusty Hardanger and three-year-old Ida Thompson bouncing on his ankle, giggling and singing along. "Don't say no! Here we go. Ride across the plain!" It was the last she would remember of her grandfather, yet the song and the smile that accompanied it were her treasured memories forever and ever and ever.

Let the singing begin.

When she was nine, Ida's daddy came home with a flivver long enough for all the children, family, neighbors, pets, and supplies; two seats forward and a jump seat in back. Let the singing begin. "Over the river and through the woods," "I love to go a wandering," even "Found a peanut, found a peanut, found a peanut last night!" It wasn't a road trip. It was a songfest. "Vallyeree! Vallyerah!" Once Ida's brother Jeffrey sang, "One Hundred Bottles of Beer on the Wall" for sixty-four enthusiastic verses before Mother cut him off with thirty-six bottles still on the wall. Everybody sang "A-a-a-men! A-a-a-men! A-ay-men! A-men! A-men!" just like Sidney Portier.

Donald Kittleson took Ida to a movie while she was still a teenager. After the *Bridge On the River Kwai* finally blew, Donald thought that "Colonel

Bogey's March" should be their song. Ida couldn't get home fast enough. Although she quickly forgot Donnie Kittleson she could forever effortlessly whistle "Colonel Bogey's March" and often did as she walked to town or later, when she shepherded her own children from school to church to home and such. They learned to whistle it too.

Things had been different when Joseph Thompson asked Ida to the Junior Prom. He was a senior and when the little band slowed down to play "I'll be seeing you in all the old familiar places…" it really did become *their* song. It played on the radio the night before Joe went off to France and Belgium. It played in Ida's head and heart until he came home again. It was a celebration of their dedication to one another. At the wedding "Ave Maria" and "The Lord's Prayer" were sung by Ida's best friend Rosalie, who could really soar on the high notes. "True Love," sung by Joe's buddy Tom was, well, sincere. Still, at the reception it was "I'll Be Seeing You" that really celebrated their special love.

Family followed. Lullabies were sung all over again. Nursery rhymes and games like "Pony girl! Pony girl! Won't you be my pony girl?" Endless refrains of "Pomp and Circumstance" at graduations, "We've Only Just Begun" and "Climb Every Mountain." There were more road trips with a new generation of "Found a Peanut" and "One Hundred Bottles of Beer on the Wall." Joe must have taught them. There were protest songs when the kids came home from college like, "Where Have All The Flowers Gone?" "Imagine" "War! Huh! What is it good for?" and "We Shall Overcome." "Where do they learn this stuff?" asked Joe. "I don't know, Joe. I just don't know," answered Ida, hiding her contented smile.

As everybody got older "How Great Thou Art" and "Unclouded Day" were comforting at teary funerals, including Joe's, and yes, eventually even Ida's. "Amazing grace, how sweet the sound…"

Before Ida passed away, a woman in the hospice by the name of Justice made the final moments more beautiful as she played her guitar at Ida's bedside. When at last they closed the lid on the casket that contained her remains and carried her from the church, one of Ida Thompson's own grandchildren picked up her grandfather's old Hardanger fiddle and played a creaky version of "Peace Like A River," then eased into a gentler version of "I'll Be Seeing You." It was a celebration of a lovely life. A celebration made memorable by the music that Ida and all of us celebrate every day of our lives.

Music is so important.

America Sings!
With Mac Huff

We gather here together to sing in harmony.
There's no one who I'd rather have standing here with me.
So put your hands together and raise them to the sky.
We can make a difference at least I know we'll try.
America Sings!

From the shore of the Pacific to the rugged coast of Maine,
The roar is just terrific aboard our freedom train.
We come because we're caring, we gather 'cause we're free.
With love and hope for sharing, from sea to shining sea.
America Sings!

America Sings!
From the mighty Mississippi, America hears the children call.
America lives in the hearts of all the people.
America! One and for all!

America Sings!
America cries.
America hopes,
America tries.

From the warmth of Arizona, to a cold Dakota snow.
From the lakes of Minnesota to the Gulf of Mexico.
From the tundra of Alaska, warm messages we bring.
From the wonders of Nebraska you will hear our voices ring.
America Sings!

WHY I LOVE MUSIC

Here is why I love to move to the music. A couple of years before I was born my mother was stricken with polio. It was feared that she would never walk again. I don't remember that of course, but I do remember an important part of her recovery process. She had some of those old records, they weren't old at the time, but they came with a book of pictures and instructions. They consisted of a lady named Miss Julie dressed in a leotard leading the listener through a series of stretches and exercises to keep the listener physically fit, or in my mother's case, to help her to walk again after her terrible illness. My mother's recovery took years. This was a long time ago, but I remember as though it were yesterday all of my brothers and sisters and I getting right down on the floor with my mother and Miss Julie and lifting our legs across our bodies, stretching this way and that way. We did sit-ups and legs-ups, the bicycle move and all sorts of other exercises to build my mother's strength. It wasn't work. It was fun. We were with our mom.

Besides helping our mother with her recovery, each of my siblings got in the habit of doing regular exercise. (Although several of them threatened me when I suggested that I was going to put full-length pictures of them alongside this chapter!) But seriously, exercise was a part of life, like brushing your teeth or combing your hair, like putting on your shoes or eating your daily breakfast. The habits that you learn as a child tend to continue as you grow into a youth and then to an adult. Guess what, my brothers and sisters and I still brush our teeth, we still comb our hair, put on our shoes, eat breakfast, and, as we did with Miss Julie and my mother, we still do regular exercise to keep fit and healthy. Do you know what? It's still fun. By the way, my mother still exercises regularly these many years later and she walks with little effort, unlike the doctor's dire predictions. I like to think we helped.

Another lesson I learned pretty early on is the power of music in any learning process. Can you think of a single child that didn't learn the alphabet singing "ABCDEFGHIJKLMNOP..." and so on? I remember a song we used to sing to learn the names of the states called the "Fifty Nifty," or one on that old TV show *School House Rock* where we learned how a bill got through Congress.

I once wrote a little musical with my friend Roger Emerson called, *The Musical Adventures of Lewis and Clark*. It was meant for elementary children to rehearse and perform as they studied the lives of those early explorers. I'll never forget the sixth grade classroom teacher who came to the music room and asked with genuine amazement, "What in the world are you teaching here in this room?" I asked her, "What do you mean?" She said, "Well today we started our unit on explorers and I asked all of the sixth graders if any of them knew anything about Meriwether Lewis and William Clark. Immediately, the entire class started singing, "It was eighteen four not a day before I left my home and family ..." For the rest of their lives those kids are going to remember the fact that Lewis and Clark began their trip to the West in eighteen hundred and four! What you learn through music you don't forget.

Let me jump to my point, and I do have one! We all know that exercise is good for you whether you are four or eighty-four. In a land that is sedentary at best, we need to learn ways to take care of ourselves physically, mentally, and even emotionally. When I was a kid that meant exercising with my mom and hearing my dad say, "Go outside and play." We tore around the neighborhood with all of the other kids until we were totally spent. It's more difficult to do that these days. Some of us live in neighborhoods where we can't simply say, "take it outside." Not to mention the fact that there are so many sedentary activities readily available: television, video games, too much homework, junk food (is that an activity?). Well, you get the idea. But we know that somewhere, somehow we still need physical activity to maintain a healthy life. It doesn't take a brain surgeon to confirm that we feel better physically *and* emotionally when we are involved in regular physical activity.

So we can all agree that children need to learn the importance of doing physical activity. Also, we all agree that what we learn through music we don't forget. Therefore I don't believe that it is at all a stretch to suggest that if we are able to get children happily involved in physical activity through music, they'll begin to develop the habits and recognize the benefits of a life-long commitment to physical activity. They'll remember the lessons just like they'll remember the alphabet. And they'll have fun doing it!

There's another point I have to bring up. Wow! Two points in one sitting! Children and adults are bombarded every day with negativity. Some of it is in the music they listen to and *think* they love. This negativity has a long lasting effect on kids and their feelings about themselves and the world around them. As people who love music and the power it can have over our lives and learning, I believe in fighting back. At least we can counterbalance some of that input with positive music. Singing and moving to songs with upbeat messages can help children feel better about their world and themselves. They can pursue happiness and with our adult guidance, get on the right path. Remember, if they learn a song or dance that makes them feel valued as a human being and helps them recognize that they are a precious member of the human race, they might just remember it as they go through the trying years of teenage-dom and beyond. Remember ABCDE-FGHIJKLMNOP...?"

What we learn through music we don't forget.

We've all been deluged of late with the reports of how overweight and out of shape our children are. Some of the statistics are staggering. Parents, grandparents, teachers and other adults are worried sick about what is happening to our kids. Some of us may even feel guilty that we have not been effective enough in teaching the children in our own lives the necessity of maintaining a steady routine of healthy diet and exercise. We don't have time. We're exhausted ourselves by what it takes to get along in the world and so on and on. Guilt won't help. Action will. Gosh! I sound like Harold Hill!

If a three or four-year-old, or even a ten-year-old gets excited about music and movement and sees it as a part of their everyday routine, they can begin to develop and internalize the healthy habits for a lifetime, just like brushing their teeth. You lead them to it, show that it's necessary and they'll do the rest.

To be frank, the best way for adults to get children to buy into something is to do it with them and to show a genuine enthusiasm for the task at hand. Your attempt at getting children to "move to the music" will work better if you show an interest in it, especially at the outset. Jump in with both feet and bring your children along with you. That really doesn't mean that you have to sing and dance to every song you introduce to your students. (You can if you want to and I believe you'll feel young again if you do.) But at least show your children that you are excited about their involvement in the activity by being there with them, encouraging them, applauding their efforts, egging them on, holding them during the swaying songs, showing them through your interest that you care about them. Your attention, along with the music and the moves, will make them feel valued. And they won't forget it.

I have taught music and dance to children for almost twenty-five years. I have written more songs for kids than I can remember, and I have loved every minute of it. In all those years it has never been my goal to use beautiful children to make beautiful music. On the contrary, it has always been my dream and I think my reality to use beautiful music to help make beautiful children.

There is no way that the music teacher can solve the problems of overweight and out of shape children in our land. But we can help. We can be one step in the right direction. We can do better by our kids, and we can do it together.

Music in My Soul

With Mac Huff

Listen to me children, I've got something to say.
There's a voice inside me that won't go away.
Finest kind of feelin's got me singin' today.
I got Music in My Soul.

People hear me hummin' and they wonder "why?'
Rhythm keeps a comin' that I can't deny.
Feet just keep a tappin', I don't even try.
I got Music in My Soul.

I got music deep inside.
A celebration I can't hide.
A joyful noise is fin'lly here to stay,
keeps me singing for a happy day.
O Happy Day!

Grab a little melody from deep in your heart.
Never been a better day for you to start.
Never keep a singer and a song apart.
I got music!
I got Music in My Soul.

Hallelu! Hallelu!
Sing hallelujah!
Jubilation! What a morning.
Sound the trumpet! Send a warning.
Beat the drums and let the cymbals ring!
Love is all around me when I sing!

I got music!
I got music!
I got Music in My Soul!
Hallelu!

IT'S ABOUT RESPECT

Despite his name, Joey Darling was not as easy to like as some kids. He didn't have an adorable giggle or a naturally cuddly nature that would make friends easily with his peers or soften the hearts of wary adults. Some might say that he was awkward looking, but they could say that about a lot of children. So, Joey really wasn't all that different from the rest. Joey was, in retrospect, quite ordinary and in itself that's not so bad. Most children don't really think of themselves as different or special until something different or special about them is pointed out.

It's about respect, so check it out, check it out!
It's about respect, ch-check it out.

On the playground during the early part of second grade Joey found himself swinging upside down on the lower rungs of a shiny jungle gym set. The upper bars above him were occupied by a small group of sixth graders each feeling their oats, as sixth graders are more than anxious to do. Hanging on the jungle gym during recess, Joey learned a naughty word. During nutrition snack that very afternoon, Joey tried out his new vocabulary. Two girls shrieked, six boys snickered, Tommy Thompson cried, and Mary Beth Bleater told the teacher. Suddenly, Joey Darling did not feel ordinary. With one well-timed expletive, Joey Darling was special.

It worked again in fourth grade, when Joey's vocabulary expanded and four letter words could be strung together in phrases that would shock a Marine. From TV, movies, CDs, and magazines (not to mention the latest group of saucy sixth graders), Joey mastered the nasty, angry sounds of gutter lingo. And oh, the attention he received! What's a little detention when your very words can make girls shriek and your best friends snicker? What's a little mark on your report card in the "considers the feelings of others" column when what you say gets such a profound reaction from those whose attention you adore?

By their sophomore year, Joey's classmates were all similar in many ways, sharing similar parent relations, fickle peer communication, and basic battles with their complexions and so on. But who wants to be similar when you are used to being special? Joey had much more to offer! So, being somewhat musically inclined, Joey started a garage band with four of his edgy sophomore friends. They called themselves "Joey and the Shockers." But to their dismay, after weeks of practice, the group was getting very little attention. They needed to do something that would set them apart.

So, Joey and the Shockers entered the Blue Lake Teenage Battle of the Bands and swore their heads off. After an opening number in which Joey screamed obscenities, denouncing every audience member from the English teacher to the Catholic priest, the band transitioned seamlessly into an identical sounding second piece in which he blasted jocks, cheerleaders, band students, and even the PTA with verbiage of violence that would cause a convict to blush. By the end of the set Joey was being tossed about in the jubilant frenzy of a mosh pit, buoyed up by many of the very people he was bashing from the stage.

By his twentieth birthday, Joey had left the Shockers, changed his name to Aybeeceedee or Elemeno, or something original like that, and was making millions with Grammy® Award-winning CDs and videos that encouraged violence against women, gays, policemen, clergy, puppies and little baby ducks. "Daring satire!" adult critics raved, afraid to be like their parents who thought the Beatles were the beginning of the end. "Ingenious Athletic Rhyming Schemes," "Freedom of Speech," and "You're Just Too Old To Get It" the headlines blared.

I do not like the kind of music that Aybeeceedee or Elemeno screams, and here is why. It hurts people. I have listened to some of it. I have asked students to explain it to me, and I respect their answers. They tell me that most of the songs have a line or two that give them a satirical twist and may even have a socially redemptive quality to them. They may have a point. But, it takes a very sophisticated ear to discern that redemptive quality, and that is not who is listening to this music. Too often the listeners are like the second graders in Joey's class. They only hear the words that are naughty to their ears. They snicker nervously at the taunts, the threats, and the exhortations to violence. They witness the attention that the naughtiness provides. A second or fourth grader, a high school sophomore, or even an adult, does not always discern the nuance of a satirical twist and embrace the veiled subliminal message of redemption.

Now don't get me wrong. Although I do not like this music, nor do I understand the accolades the performers receive because of it, I absolutely believe that they have a right to perform it, sell it, and wallow in it if they so choose. But every time I see that Mr. ExYZeRo sells another bazillion CDs, it makes me that much more convinced that as teachers, we need to buck up and balance the field of what's going in and what's coming out of our students hearts, minds and mouths. There have always been tyrants who use the power of music for their own advancement to the detriment of eager listeners looking for direction. Sometimes even very good music has been used for that purpose. Think of Hitler's use of Wagner in the bolstering of the misguided Nazi spirit.

Point this out to your students. Don't dismiss their opinions outright, and certainly don't pretend that this music doesn't exist. Denial is not a valid tool of education. Make them defend their position when they say they relate to something that you find offensive. Ask a young woman what she gets out of listening to a "song" that berates women. Ask a young man to explain to you the thrill of listening to someone who encourages violence against any figure of authority. Listen carefully. They will have opinions about the song's use of sarcasm and irony as the tools of an expressive artist. Give them an honest ear. And then teach them the fourth verse of "America, the Beautiful."

> *O Beautiful for patriot dream*
> *That sees beyond the years.*
> *Thine alabaster cities gleam*
> *Undim'd by human tears.*

With the power of good music and texts, we have our own arsenal to utilize against the loose-lipped vitriol of those who would use that power for exploitation. We are not going to roll over and let hate and greed usurp the positive influence that we know music can play in the minds of children and adults alike. Look out, Mr. PeeQueAreEss! Music teachers of the world have more than a few weapons of our own in the form of beauty, power, grace and intelligence. It will be in the music we teach every single day. It will be in the songs our children memorize and internalize every time we have contact with them. And when they are old enough to discern what is good and bad, naughty or nice, they will know the difference.

It's about respect …

The Sea Is So Wide

With Mac Huff

(To Marian Wright Edelman and the Children's Defense Fund)

Dear Lord be good to me.
Dear Lord watch over me.
Dear Lord hear my prayer.

The sea is so wide, my boat is so small.
Dear Lord, I stand amazed at the wonder of it all.
Adrift on a rolling sea with no guiding star in sight.
I feel so alone in the darkness of the night.

What I need is your hand. Will you walk by my side?
And see me as I am, my arms are open wide.
We can hope and we can dream for the dawning of a brighter day.
Dear Lord, be good to me and help me find my way, I pray.

Lost in the stars that glow thru' the blackness of night.
Each star is blessed with a wish of radiant light.
Like so many stars,
There are so many people whose dreams need a spark to shine.
If I stumble will someone hold on?
Falling stars are forgotten by dawn.
Will someone hear my cry?
Will someone ask the world "why?"
Will someone take the time
To watch the sky?

Dear Lord! Dear Lord!
The sea is so wide, my boat is so small.
Dear Lord, I stand amazed at the wonder of it all.
So shine your light throughout the world and bring me home to stay.
Dear Lord, be good to me, this is all I ask, and all I pray.

Dear Lord,
Be good to me.

FAMILY HISTORY MONTH

In October we celebrate Family History Month. We contemplate our roots and learn more about ourselves by looking at our own unique heritage. We remember the lives of our ancestors and celebrate immediate "families" with whom we share today. Family. What a word. What a concept. I'm not sure a concise definition even exists. If it does, it must be the broadest explanation Webster ever created. I have yet to see any two "families" even remotely identical, they're like snowflakes and pirouettes.

Those of you who know me know that my own family is a real doozie! (Doozie is a word that comes somewhere between do and re in a future edition of a revised version of a *Progressive Dictionary of Contemporary Music*.) Like many people in the United States, my great-grandparents made the arduous sail across the ocean and immediately began to help populate their new home with huge families. They took this role very seriously. My father was one of ten children, most of whom became teachers, and my mother (also a teacher) was an only child. They went on to have ten more of their own. I'm the sixth; "John the VI," I like to claim. All of us became teachers and most married teachers, now begetting teachers in a new generation. It's a lovely affliction our family shares. Referring to my relations, a friend recently remarked, "That's not a family, it's a clan!" I decided to take it as a compliment, even though I think that "faculty" may have been a more accurate definition. For my father, a school superintendent, having ten children was simply job security.

With a family of that size we always had plenty of adjunct members, "brothers" and "sisters" who needed a floor to sleep on, a slice of the already multi-dissected pizza, and a family to belong to. There was the other John, the neighbor boy who just sort of moved in at age fifteen and still thinks of my parents' house as home. Wayne and Willie were the farm boys who spent more time at our house than their own because we lived close to school and my mother was willing to type their term papers. They astonished us with their appetite for food, laughter, family togetherness, and my mother's typing services. Umba, a teenager from far off Papua, New

Guinea, came for a year and stayed for seven. Believe me, there were many, many more, and each of them was "family" as well.

How many times have music students told us that the band or choir they participate in is like a family to them? In truth, during certain periods of their lives they probably spend more time with these musical "families" than they do with their blood relatives. A frightening realization strikes many music teachers when they consider the awesome role that family plays in any young person's life. It can be daunting to think that you are now expected to be chef, cook, coach, and role model to so many new students who suddenly see you as an important, maybe even parental, figure in their lives. At the same time, you are supposed to be teaching them the finer points of pitch, rhythm, harmony and all of the other subtle nuances of music.

Nowhere in your job description as a music specialist did it say that you were expected to do all of this and also become a surrogate parent to a roomful of children. Nor should it. No matter how hard you work, as a music teacher you will never be able to totally fulfill the role that true family ought to play in any child's life. This should not be expected of you.

In music everybody can find a home.

Like it or not though, as one who spends time with children exploring some of the most tender, creative elements of their being, an effective music teacher may at least be able to help them through the awkward and lonely periods they will all experience at one time or another, times during which their ears and hearts may very well be more open to your entreaties and examples than those of their actual parents. No, you cannot provide the permanence that a family ought to supply in abundance. But you can provide a venue of enlightenment and fun, a refuge from trouble, and a place to belong.

During this Family History Month, I encourage you not to give up on a child until you can honestly say, "I have given him every chance." So often I have heard stories that *a place in the choir* was the singular chance that saved a singular child. The music classroom can be a place where a wayward son or daughter temporarily finds a home. Almost every music teacher I have ever met has a story of a child who made it through the day because of the sense of being needed; learned most acutely in his or her music class.

There is a reason armies march to war to the sound of drums, movies turn to soundtracks when words fail to tell the story, and dentists drill your teeth to the sounds of your favorite compact disc for distraction. Music is part of being human, and it makes a difference in the lives of every member of the family of humankind. Now that's something to celebrate!

In music everybody can find a home. I hope that you cherish the fact that your classroom does serve a role as family. Until every woodblock is broken or every recorder is chewed to pieces, I encourage you to relish your guardian role as head of this unique, non-exclusive family. As difficult as it may be, I love the way that music teachers make certain that every member of their extended and ever growing family has *a place in the choir.*

We Are a Family

With Mac Huff

Here we stand together, a fam'ly you and I.
A fam'ly lasts forever, on this you can rely.
Together we are special, together you and me.
Standing friend to friend we'll always be a family.

A family. A family. We're all part of a family.
Can't you see, you and me?
We are family.

A family is simple, it's love that's always there.
It's people helping people and showing that you care.
So I will stand beside you, and you'll be there for me.
Wherever two are gathered you can see a family.

A family. A family. We're all part of a family.
Can't you see, you and me?
We are family.

One and one is two, two and two makes four:
Together we can always do much more, much more.

A family. A family. We're all part of a family.
Can't you see, you and me?
We are family.
We are family. We are family.

IT'S ALL ABOUT ME!

Walking through the airport I saw a beautiful young girl, probably sixteen or seventeen years old, lounging in a low airport chair. Okay, I looked. Okay, I gawked. She was a leggy beauty sure to make young men nervous and a father apoplectic. She had long and silky hair, ivory skin, bright blue eyes and perfect white teeth. Beyond that, all that I remember is that she wore a pair of black pants with white writing all over them. It was the same four and a half words over and over as clear as the skin on her face. From my vantage point it was her only blemish. "IT'S ALL ABOUT ME!" they literally stated over hip and thigh, calf and ankle. "It's all about me!" they screamed from knee to foot and knee to waist. "It's all about Me! It's all about Me! It's all about Me! Me! Me!"

"No," I thought sadly to myself as my infatuation faded. "No," I thought as I walked passed the newsstand with blaring headlines of war and terror. "No," I thought as I picked up the phone and talked to a couple of my child advocacy friends later that afternoon and was reminded that there are still two hundred thousand homeless children in America. "No," I thought when I considered the plight of the children of continents like Africa where literally millions are facing the ravages of starvation and AIDS. "No," I winced as I read about the rapidly growing gaps between our own country's haves and have-nots. No. As a child a lot is about you, and it ought to be. But it is not *all* about you. This is a country, a globe and a galaxy that you share with others. You are part of something bigger, something bigger than me, bigger than you.

I'm old enough to be able to say that when I was a little kid I raced out of the house when I heard an airplane flying over to catch a glimpse at this new and exciting invention. Blair, Wisconsin wasn't exactly on the flight path to a lot of exotic places so it was still quite a novelty for a plane to pass overhead in the 1960s. To most of us the idea of flying through the clouds was as awesome and impossible as going to the moon. Then one day we watched a man walk on the moon.

Like most Americans, I have always marveled and been inspired by space exploration. So I remember when the Challenger exploded in 1986; where I was, and how I was feeling. It was one of those seminal moments like the day President Kennedy was assassinated or terrorists flew into the World Trade Center. Recently we lost another space shuttle directly over our Texan skies. I was in Ushuaia, Argentina, the southern-most city in the world that day when I heard the news. People there grieved too. It was all about them too.

I have heard people suggest that perhaps manned space travel is inappropriate, that we flirt with challenging the heavens where only God should dwell and we should watch. I don't believe this to be true.

I believe that the God-given human ingenuity that allows eight human astronauts to board a small vehicle, break through our protective atmosphere and soar among the stars helps us all to be better for ourselves and by each other. As they whirl around our tiny planet we are inspired to see ourselves as a part of something more than we often do. We are more than individuals. We are more than Americans. We are more than earthlings. We are a part of something greater than we can possibly understand. The idea and reality of exploring the heavens can do that.

Can we use music to nurture givers as opposed to takers?

Music can do that too. With inspired harmonies and impassioned melodies we are able to transcend time and space and even the confines of our humanness, and soar like astronauts a bit closer to infinity. We are part of something bigger than ourselves and I believe we are more able to find joy in the awesome and peace with the Impossible.

Can we use music to teach young and impressionable minds that indeed it is not "all about me?" Can we use their *place in the choir* as an opportunity to demonstrate that it is indeed preferable to live a life that is not "all about me?" Can we use music to nurture givers as opposed to takers, lovers as opposed to haters, peace as opposed to turmoil?

I believe we can, and for this I am particularly grateful.

Like a Mighty Stream
With Moses Hogan

Lift ev'ry voice and let us sing!
In ev'ry song let freedom ring!
From ev'ry soul comes a noble dream.
Let justice roll like a mighty stream.

Like a Mighty Stream.
Like a Mighty Stream.
Let justice roll,
Like a Mighty Stream.

Oh ev'ry trial we'll overcome,
When ev'ry child beneath the sun,
And ev'ry soul shall live as one.
The noble dream has just begun!

Like a Mighty Stream.
Like a Mighty Stream.
Let justice roll,
Like a Mighty Stream.

2001: A CHOIR ODYSSEY

I wish we could have rigged up this chapter so that when you turned the page you heard the opening strains of Strauss' *Also Sprach Zarathustra*. After all, the real 2001 odyssey has finally begun, and by all accounts it looks like it's going to be a wild ride for music teachers. Go ahead, put the recording on full blast when you make your next entrance into the third grade music class pushing your cart full of instruments they call "the moving classroom," or as you take to the podium in the glamorous "No-Purpose Room" for your President's Day program. Go ahead. You deserve that kind of fanfare. You made it to 2001!

Strauss' tone poem is a fascinating composition which continues to prompt debate even over one hundred years after it was written. It brings into focus one of the more heated critical and philosophical debates of the nineteenth century between the proponents of program music, and those who favored so-called "absolute music;" music whose appeal is made in "strictly musical" terms. Most people today would probably agree that music is by it's very nature abstract. Sounds don't convey exact meaning the same way that words can. Music can, on the other hand, evoke feelings and associations that may be profoundly different for each and every listener. In *Also Sprach Zarathustra*, Strauss was trying to express the ideas and philosophies of Friedrich Nietsche's famous poem of the same name. (You remember Nietsche. He's the one who voiced the wonderful thought, "Without music, life would be a mistake." I also happen to know that he went on to say that he "would only believe in a God that knew how to dance!" Now here's a guy with *a place in my choir!*) Back to 2001; most people who listen to Strauss' composition probably wouldn't have a clue what Nietsche was trying to say in his writings. In fact, one critic of the time said that if old Friedrich had actually heard the piece he would have laughed himself silly! Perhaps.

Still, what a remarkable work like *Also Sprach Zarathustra* does prove is that the value of any music lies not necessarily in how accurately it paints a picture or tells a story, but in it's inherent musical qualities and it's capacity to move us. Welcome to 2001!

In January we celebrate the man and the legacy of Dr. Martin Luther King, Jr. I never got to meet Dr. King Jr. in person. I wish I could have. I did lead a bunch of young people in the Martin Luther King Parade through the streets of Atlanta, Georgia once, and have a picture of Mrs. Martin Luther King, Jr. looking over my shoulder with a look of pride as our young singers belted out the message of a song entitled "We Are One!" I am proud of that picture and proud of having been involved in such a tribute to a great American.

Music can evoke feelings and associations that may be profoundly different for each and every listener.

In addition to being a seminal leader in the civil rights movement for our nation and a devout religious leader, Dr. King understood as well as anybody the very music of the language we all use to communicate. The rhythm and melodies of his famous speeches are legendary in their ability to rouse the passions of his listeners; to heal, to inspire, to challenge. When he repeated words like "I Have A Dream!" "I Have Been to the Mountain Top!" and "Free! Free! Free at last!" he did so with tone, rhythm, and even melody that moved us in ways that only music can.

When the marchers that Dr. King led on those stormy days of our history linked arms and marched through the streets to force change where change was needed, they almost always used music to unite them and stir the hearts of all who witnessed their demonstration. The determined refrains of "We Shall Overcome" and even "Glory, Glory Hallelujah!" bolstered the courage of both participant and listener, stirring their souls to action.

I remember talking to my cousin Ellie (a teacher of course), who was lucky enough as a child to be at the Poor People's March in Washington, D.C. in 1963. This was one of the most famous events in which Dr. King spoke so eloquently, and as a result can take credit for being a catalyst that changed the world forever. Ellie bore witness to me that as well as all of the speeches, especially Dr. King's, the single most potent unifying force at this original Million People's March was the presence of music. When you stood in the shadow of the Washington Monument, elbows linked with others who fought for justice, the words "I Have a Dream" still echoing in your head, singing "Come By Here, Lord" and "We Shall Overcome," hearts simultaneously softened to the pain of the suffering poor and hardened with the determination that things were never going to be the same. Music has that kind of power. Music matched with potent poetry can change the hearts of an aching world. Dr. King knew this.

In February we celebrate the birthdays of our presidents. Many of our presidents were fine musicians in their own right. Harry Truman and Richard Nixon both played the piano. Bill Clinton wailed on the tenor sax. Of course, there also was Ulysses S. Grant who said, "I only know two songs, one is "Yankee Doodle," the other isn't." We'll skip right over him, even though I know for a fact that in the Civil War he sent his soldiers into battle to the stirring cadence of the field drums, understanding the power it could have to strengthen their reserve.

Real leaders understand the role that the arts in general and music specifically play in our ordinary, or exceptional lives. President John Adams said, "I must study politics and war that my sons may have liberty to study mathematics and philosophy ... in order to give their children a right to study painting, poetry and music."

President John Kennedy pointed out that one year, "more Americans went to symphony concerts than went to baseball games. This may be viewed as an alarming statistic, but I think that both baseball and the country will endure." Frankly, Mr. President, your point strengthens my faith in the future of American culture.

And President Thomas Jefferson called music ... "the favorite passion of my soul." Mine too, Mr. Jefferson! Here, here, Mr. Adams and Mr. Kennedy! Thank you Dr. King! Welcome one and all to 2001 and an odyssey in music!

Revolution of the Heart

With Mark Brymer

A change is happ'n'in' all around;
the pace is racin', causin' my pulse to pound.
Deep in my soul I hear an awesome sound, a revolution!

Keep goin' strong, don't be denied.
This is the call, it's ours if we only try.
There's never been a better battle cry, a revolution!

Now is the time, this is the place to start.
You can win if you just listen to your heart!

Love! Can you give it? I can give it!
Peace! Can you live it? I can live it!
Joy! Can you feel it? I can feel it!
I've got the constitution, for a Revolution of the Heart!

Your life will never be the same.
When your heart's your guide, life's just a game.
Yes, open minds are gonna fan the flames of revolution!

We're all for one, living one for all,
When all dividing walls begin to fall.
Together we can rise and answer the call of revolution!

Now is the time, this is the place to start.
You can win if you just listen to your heart!

Love! Can you give it? I can give it!
Peace! Can you live it? I can live it!
Joy! Can you feel it? I can feel it!
I've got the constitution for a Revolution of the Heart!

I'LL MAKE A DIFFERENCE

It is Mardi Gras time in New Orleans. Party time. As I write this chapter the horrors of Hurricane Katrina are just beginning to be realized by the people of America's Gulf Coast Region. As we reel from these stark realities it doesn't seem an ideal time to stage a parade or dance in the streets. We feel for the hundreds of thousands of people affected by this tragedy and wonder how on earth we shall ever recover. We have been inundated with news clips and articles documenting the unfathomable devastation and realize that we will be witnessing this for years to come as the area works to recover from this tragedy.

> *How wonderful it is that nobody need wait a single moment before starting to improve the world.* —Anne Frank

When musicians think about New Orleans our first thoughts are of the French Quarter, jazz, blues, and the great figures that made New Orleans famous for its music. People like Louis Armstrong, the Marsalis family, the Preservation Hall Band. Now it's difficult to think about that joyous New Orleans and its famous Mardi Gras after what it has just endured. Being somewhat familiar with New Orleans through friends and visits, I am confident that with the indomitable spirit of its citizens, even this year, endure they shall. Despite the catastrophe there will be parties and yes, even music when Mardi Gras time rolls around. Still, in the wake of Katrina we focus first on the amazing national outpouring of care, courage, and generosity that has been displayed in the aftermath of our shared disaster. When one American hurts, we all hurt.

Out of calamity it is encouraging to witness our human potential for sharing and caring. It has been inspiring to watch how many citizens of our land have been so willing and eager to reach their hand into the darkness people have been forced to live in and help guide them into the light. People are so good. At their core, people are so very good.

My friend Moses Hogan was from New Orleans. Many times before he passed away a few years ago we talked together about his love for the city he called home and for the friends and family that shared it with him. It seems appropriate then, that as his hometown suffers we include here one of his most inspiring songs, calling on all of us to do something to make a positive difference in our world. In little or grand ways we can make our world better if we all decide to do so, one person, one deed, one idea at a time.

I'm the one who can make the difference,
Yes, I will make the difference;
Against all odds,
I can live to share my life with others,
Yes, I will make the difference,
I can make it!
Take my hand as we make this journey across the land.

I had courage to keep goin' on.
I had faith when all hope was gone.
I had the strength to keep holding on
I can make the difference,
I can make the difference,
I can make the difference
Yes I can!

We're the ones who can make the difference,
Yes, we will make the difference;
Against all odds,
We can live to share our love with others,
Yes, we will make the difference,
We can make it!
Take my hand as we make this journey across the land.

We will make it! Take my hand!

As teachers we often encourage our students to go out and make a difference in their world. We have been told that indeed one person can do just that. Do we really believe it? Especially when problems seem so overwhelming, do we really think that one small individual can have an impact?

Have you ever lain awake on a summer night when all is still except for the insistent, aggravating, annoying, frustrating, irritating, infuriating, maddening, (I'm almost through the thesaurus) buzz of a single mosquito who has discovered you and liked your taste? It is proof that someone very, very small can make a huge difference in the world of another.

From my point of view there is no greater joy or satisfaction in life than that incredible feeling of having the power to make the world different, to plant a tree even though you may never sit in its shade, because you know that the next generation will be cooled by your efforts. Everybody has that power, but not everybody recognizes it. One of the great missions we have as teachers is to hold up the mirror to our students and show them that they are valuable and that they too can find joy and fulfillment in service to others. In our role as teachers one of our main objectives ought to be to teach students of all ages that a life of giving is truly a life worth living.

But how do we do that? In a world filled with consumerism in which all are bombarded with messages of "every man for himself," "he who dies with the most toys wins" and so on, how do we convince people that a worthy life is best made up of helping others as we help ourselves?

Well, as we all know, the most effective teaching is often accomplished through demonstration. Do as I do.

I witness one person making a difference every time I watch a dedicated teacher doing their job. You buzz like mosquitoes. You are pushers. Okay, nudgers. You nudge your students along. And each little nudge pushes them closer to being more productive members of society. When you nudge them toward the recognition of their own worth as individuals who can change their world, you help them discover a life of genuine value in the same way that you found value in your chosen profession as a nudger, a pusher, a world changer, a teacher. Confucius said,

> *To put the world right in order, we must first put the nation in order;*
> *to put the nation in order, we must first put the family in order;*
> *to put the family in order, we must first cultivate our personal life;*
> *we must first set our hearts right.*

That's what you do as teachers every day. You try to set straight the hearts and minds of each individual student knowing that through them, one by one, you have the power to make the world a better place. When you reveal to young people the riches they possess as movers and shakers of their world you nudge the world in the best of ways. You may not reach them all, but the ones you do will be your legacy and your "difference."

Sometimes it can all seem so overwhelming. Obviously when hundreds of thousands of people are displaced by a hurricane this seems an understatement. Even in a classroom of a few dozen students the challenge of making a difference in anybody's world can seem a daunting task indeed. A few months ago I went to church at the First Presbyterian Church of Encino, California. Behind me sat John Wooden, the famous basketball coach and guru to many. I was reminded of something he once said about making a difference. "Do not let what you cannot do interfere with what you can do."

Do not allow yourself to be overwhelmed by the tasks that lie ahead. Be a mosquito and just keep buzzing. To make a difference we all just need to keep plugging away, not letting what we *can't* do interfere with what we most certainly *can* do. As teachers we do this every day. We shall not be overwhelmed. We can make a difference every single day. What a grand lesson to teach our students in the classroom, on the playground, on the streets, or in the choir.

Miracles

With Mark Brymer

Willa Cather, one of the most interesting
women writers in American literary history once wrote,
"Where there is great love, there will always be miracles."

On a new day in a new way,
Wakes an old world ready to believe again.
With a fresh start, and a brave heart,
A breath of hope determined to achieve again.
Ev'ry sunrise brings the promise of a new day.
We can see, if we realize there is a way.

Where there is great love, there will always be miracles,
miracles, miracles.
Where there is great love, there will always be miracles.

Just imagine love unending.
With the power of our hearts united.
When ev'ry heart beat, like the rising sun;
Feels the light of love that is ignited.
Feel the strength compassion brings to all mankind.
From this moment to forever, one thing you'll find.

Where there is great love, there will always be miracles,
miracles, miracles.
Where there is great love, there will always be miracles.

BEACONS OF HOPE

I am lucky to live on a ranch in the boonies. And on that ranch there lives a cow, E-I-E-I oops! Sorry, that is not at all where that was supposed to go. What I wanted to tell you is that because I live on a ranch in the boonies, you can walk outside in the middle of a December night (which in the boonies in December is shortly after lunch), and especially when there is no moon, see stars that would make you wilt with humility. I come from a family of stargazers. Oh, not the kind that can name ninety-nine constellations and explain the difference between a quasar and a nebulae. In fact, other than the Big Dipper, I mostly just see leopards and ladybugs, Dalmatians and anything else with spots. I once thought I saw a UFO but then it landed and my Aunt Caroline got out, as real as ever. But on clear nights my family and I gaze up with incomprehension, much like I do at algebra, agape with awe and wonder until our necks are sore and our noses are running. Then we go inside and consider, "Just how small are we?"

There is a light in December that pierces the darkness and inspires the hearts of celebrants all over the world, people of different faiths, backgrounds, races, colors, and creeds. There is a light in December. See how it flickers from the hand of the one who wields the Shamash and lights the candles of the Menorah. See the soft glow from the terra cotta luminarias. Look at the rays beaming from the flickering Kinara. See the Star in the East over Bethlehem. There are beacons of light in the December sky that cause many of us to contemplate the incomprehensible and find peace with the impossible.

And in every case, they are lights that provide inspiration, comfort, and most of all, hope.

There are also beacons of light here on Earth that exude a totally different level of inspiration and hope. They are the human stars that shine in our lives and help us to do better by each other and ourselves. They are our lighthouses in the storm, our pillars of fire in the desert. They are the lights that help us see that we have purpose, that we have potential, that we have promise. Sometimes these lights are parents or siblings. Sometimes they are public figures, poets, artists, ministers, strangers, or friends. Always, they are teachers.

Teachers. Purveyor's of dreams, beacons of hope to so many, stars in the eyes of their students. You've had them. You've been them. You realize that in order to help your gazers reach for the stars it is not enough to simply send them to a computer and ask them to retrieve information. They only need a modem for that. You know that it is the inspiration you provide through your example, your enthusiasm, your professionalism, your genuine concern, your preparedness, your shine, that makes you more than a drill sergeant, more than an almost life-like show in a planetarium. It is your training, your calling, and your genuine star qualities that make you the real thing.

A teacher is a beacon of hope to so many.

Like the lights of December, a teacher is a beacon of hope to so many. Although the road is sometimes dark and even sinister, you persevere. You keep offering hope and keep hoping yourself. You keep believing in and even loving the students that are sometimes difficult to believe in and even more difficult to love. You keep shining for them, even when you're tired, even when the administration, parents, town folk, and even puppies seem unfair to you. When demands are greater and budgets non-existent, you shine. When you have to clean your own classroom, your own family is neglected because of your schedule, you doubt your very own worth and effectiveness, you still shine, because there are those who need your light.

There is a phrase I have loved. I always assumed it was from the Bible. It isn't. (Doesn't that kind of revelation just frost ya?) Well, it could have been. Maybe it was in one of the scrolls that got lost. But what a thought! I suppose it was intended as a reference to the light of God. So be it. But it must also apply to the brave luminescence of the earthbound teacher, who bucks up and shines day after day, year after year, who knows in their heart of hearts that this is the day that at least one of their students will need to gaze upon a real, live beacon of hope. And you will be it, the light, the beacon, the star.

"And the darkness cannot put out it out!"

Especially in December.

Children of the Earth
With Mac Huff

Listen to the whispers of the land. They grow from humble soil.
Listen as it calls in quiet storms, offspring of nature's toil.
Oh my people do you see, oh my people do you hear,
Oh my people can you live together?
Let's live together, children of the earth.

Children of the earth cry out!
Children of the earth cry out!
Daughters of the sun and moon, sons of a shining star.
Listen to the land, listen to the land,
The land remembers.

Listen to the sigh of shooting stars, the silence of falling stones.
Listen to the roar of shifting sand, a voice that calls us home.
Oh my people do you see,
Oh my people do you hear?
Oh my people can you live together?
Let's live together, children of the earth.

We were born as one with open hearts and open minds.
We grew as one for all mankind,
Like morning sun, we're rays of hope,
Born to shine together.
Let's live together!

Children of the earth cry out!
Children of the earth cry out!
Daughters of the sun and moon, sons of a shining star.
Listen to the land, listen to the land,
The land remembers.

THERE IS A SOUND I LOVE

There is a sound I love. It is the sound of children laughing. Giggles and blasts, snickers and snorts, I love their laughs so honest, so true. What can be more pleasurable than the cackles of a child being tossed into the air by their father, or tickled to the point of nearly silent, open-mouthed guffaws by an uncle that doesn't realize what might come out next if he doesn't stop? If you've never been in a theater where children fall off their seats with laughter at the silliest movie, or amidst a game of peek-a-boo full of squeals and peals, you have not heard the chuckles of angels. For it is the laugh of a child that makes me smile. There is a sound I love. It is the sound of children laughing.

You cannot hear the sound of children singing and fail to think that this is a world worth preserving.

There is a sound I love. It is the sound of children playing. Is there a better sound on the planet than the one you hear when you walk past an elementary school during recess? It is the sound of many balls bouncing, ropes being twirled and skipped, shrieks and howls, hollers and hoots from beautiful beings finally allowed to use their "outside voices." "I'm open! I'm open!" cries the three-foot-three tight end. "Ollie, Ollie, in free," "red rover, red rover," "Duck! Duck! Goose!" mingles together with the general cacophony that makes even the dreariest asphalt dance with light and life. Is it possible that we forget the games of life as we get older? Do we forget to jump rope, avoid the cracks, skip instead of walk? Do we forget to make the sounds of the playground during recess? There is a sound I love. It is the sound of children playing.

There is a sound I love. It is the sound of children praying. "Now I lay me down to sleep," so honest, so true; unencumbered by the weight of adulthood and the trappings of judgment, they pray with an earnestness often misplaced by adults. "I pray the Lord my soul to keep," a child's prayer seems headed directly to the Source, free from static, free from bargaining, free from fear. "If I should die before I wake," they take it so personally, "I pray the Lord My soul to take," with thoughts so simple, so candid, so clean. Is it possible that as adults we forget the simplicity and the power of solemn prayer? Do we become so cynical that we think only of hedging our bets, calling in favors, forgetting the Power? There is a sound I love. It is the sound of children praying.

There is a sound I love. It is the sound of children singing. Alone or together, raucous or sublime they offer a sound to melt the hearts of the world's most cantankerous. Perhaps it is because we know that it is so fleeting. Like the rising of the phoenix it lives so splendidly and then is gone, in the child's case, forever. The song from a child, when shared with the world rivals the meadowlark, surpasses the wren. It is a gift to all who have outgrown it. You cannot hear the sound of children singing and fail to think that this is a world worth preserving. You cannot hear their song and not assume the mantle of protecting them from all that would drown them out. You cannot love a child and not encourage them to find their voice and sing their song. There is a sound I love. It is the sound of children laughing, playing, praying, and perhaps most of all, singing.

Child Song

There is a voice that can be heard
When the darkest night carries over to sunrise,
When the shadows of fear and doubt
Spread their sinister fingers over man and beast.
There is a voice piercing the cold of despair,
The heat of frustration, the weariness of maturity,
The loneliness of what it can be to be human.
There is voice that sings "good morning"
Even when it is anguished.
"Good morning" even when dawn is desolate,
"Good morning" even when it is night.
There is a voice that doesn't know cynicism,
That hasn't learned to hate,
That will not lose hope, that never gives up.
There is a voice. I hear it everyday.

THINGS THAT CAN'T BE TAUGHT IN MUSIC CLASS

I decided to sit down and make a list of all the things that cannot be taught in music class. I was thinking that an obvious place to start would be by going through the rest of the school day and examining the other required subjects. There must be a reason we have all these other classes. It must be that these are subjects that cannot be taught and learned in the music classroom. That's right, they must be outside the music curriculum.

I started with math. But after careful consideration I realized no, math is not outside the music curriculum. In many ways math and music are not very far apart at all. In music we teach children about division every time we demonstrate that a whole note is made up of two half notes, or four quarter notes, eight eighth notes, and on and on. We can use a triplet to show how three can divide one. We teach ratios and fractions, addition and subtraction, multiplication, and a slew of other "tions" every day in music class. No, math cannot be on the list. Math can certainly be taught through music.

Okay, history. Nobody is using music class to teach about history. But then again, that's not actually the case, is it? As I stated previously, one of my favorite stories is the true story of the sixth grade classroom teacher who cornered the music teacher in the teacher's workroom, and said, "What on earth are you singing about down there in that boiler room you call a music facility?"

"What do you mean?" replied the coy music teacher.

"Well, I asked all of my sixth graders if any of them knew anything about the explorers Lewis and Clark as we were beginning our unit on westward expansion. Without even a count off the entire class sang, "It was eighteen four not a day before they left their home and families…." complete with choreography and suggestions for costuming!"

You see the sixth grade was presenting a musical called *The Adventures of Lewis and Clark* and were already full of historical facts they had learned through the songs included in their program. History can indeed be taught through music. It's off the list.

Geography. There you go, geography cannot be taught through music. Hmm. Yet I've heard children name all of the United States in that song

"Fifty Nifty." Surely, it would not be a big step to assume that this would also lead them to a map to discover where these places are. Not only that, who would know anything about Flagstaff, Winona, Kingman, Barstow, and San Bernardino if they never sang the song "Route 66?" No, geography can certainly be taught through music. Strike it.

English cannot be taught through music. Of course, I do remember an absolutely remarkable experience I had when I visited Hollywood High School in Hollywood, California. Most people know it by some of its most famous graduates like Carol Burnett and James Garner. In more recent years as the city has changed it has become the home of students from all over the world as the melting pot that is America is lived out near Hollywood and Vine. I was privileged to work with the choirs of that school one day and then spent an hour or so with the English as a Second Language Chorus. I am not exaggerating when I tell you that there were twenty-three different languages counted as first languages among the forty some students in the class. Still, they all came together in the ESL choir and had an opportunity to practice their adopted English language through song in a joyful, non-threatening environment. They practiced diction. They expanded their vocabulary. They broadened their understanding of our American culture and added to it with their effort and insight. Not only that, they were teaching each other songs from their own native lands and in the languages of their people. So, not only was English being learned and reinforced, but other languages were being introduced and explored all through music. English has to be taken off the list. For that matter, even in traditional American choirs students are singing in languages from all over the world. Italian, French, German, and Latin songs are a great part of our choral tradition and a great way to begin to learn another language. Also, with the intense interest these days in World Music, more exotic and even obscure languages are being sung and celebrated in our music classes everyday. So foreign language cannot be on the list of things that cannot be taught in music class. *Togliere esso l'elenco! Nehmen Sie es ab der Liste. Le prendre de la liste!* It's gone!

One more note about that English tirade. My sister teaches high school English. She tells me that one of her most effective lessons of the year is when she has her students sing some of the great poems of the English language to the tune of a well-known song or TV theme. Once you've sung Emily Dickinson's "Because I Could Not Stop For Death" to the theme from *Gilligan's Island*, I don't think you ever forget it. She tells me she has students who have graduated many years ago, coming up to her at reunions and singing all the verses with remarkable accuracy. I wonder if they can do the same with poems they memorized without the help of a song. English is definitely off the list.

Through our music we can discover with remarkable accuracy who we were at any point in our history, and who we are today.

Social studies. Not a chance. Perhaps more than any other subject the study of society can be taught in the music classroom. Through our music we can discover with remarkable accuracy who we were at any point in our history, and who we are today. Our passions, hang-ups, hobbies, religious beliefs, goals, dreams, frustrations and party habits are celebrated in our music and have been for hundreds of years. In many ways, the study of our own society and the social organization of other societies are best examined through music and the other arts. It is through music that we can teach about who we were, are, and might become. It is through music that a child can learn that they have a place in this complex and confusing world. It is through music that a child can learn to touch, listen, hurt, feel, celebrate, and heal. It is through music that a child can learn compassion, respect, honesty, responsibility, and courage. It is through music that a child can learn to be more human. To explore music, is a social study.

Well, what has happened here? I started off trying to make a list of all of the things that cannot be taught through music and I find that I have no list at all. It may come to no surprise to most of you that in the end, there indeed is no subject that cannot be taught or at least reinforced in an engaging music classroom. Do not misunderstand. I believe very strongly that the study of music in itself is as valid as any other subject. Without music and the other arts, this world would indeed be a dull place to live or learn. We need music; all of us do. But isn't it exciting to also recognize the potential that our chosen subject has to help young people discover knowledge and expertise in all of the other subjects? Math, history, geography, English, foreign language, social studies, and so much more are what we teach when we teach music.

What are the things that cannot be taught in music class? My list is blank and I can't wait to get started!

My first big break!

Don't my cousins and brothers look thrilled to back me up?

Blair, Wisconsin's Big Budget High School Musical!

Coretta Scott King at the Martin Luther King, Jr. Parade, Atlanta, Georgia.

Hands up for America Sings!

And the wall came tumblin' down!
Berlin 1989

America Sings!
WE ARE ONE

*Children's Defense Fund
Benefit "The sea is so wide."*

*Marian Wright
Edelman and me!*

America Sings!
Nashville

America Sings! Salt Lake City

America Sings!
St. Louis

America Sings!
Chicago

America Sings!
California

America Sings!
Atlanta

Canada Sings!

*Charlie has a
place in my
choir any day!*

A DAY IN
THE LIFE

THE SUNDAY NIGHT
SYNDROME

At the start of a new year, on a birthday or the first day of school after
a summer of vacation, the annual re-evaluation of one's position in the
universe is apt to rise to the surface. Certain questions spring to the fore-
front: "You mean we have to do it again? Is this what my life is going to be
forever? What should I do with my life?" In some ways it's like what my
family of teachers wryly refer to as the "Sunday Night Syndrome," that
slightly nauseous feeling you start to get late Sunday afternoon when you
know you have to go to work again tomorrow. It really has nothing to do
with whether or not you like your job. It's just the nature of being human
to take a deep breath (or gasp), before we launch into the challenges of the
next week's adventures.

As teachers, we look to the start of another school year. It may be our first
year, maybe our thirtieth. The questions are often the same. "You mean we
have to do it again? Is this what my life is going to be forever? What should
I do with my life?" Legitimate questions, every year, every day, every hour.

We all have abilities. Some are innate, some learned. Singing,
dancing, playing sports, working with numbers, writing stories, growing
plants are some of the many, many areas in which each of us excels. It
is what you choose to do with those abilities that show the kind of
person you really are.

Most music teachers have been practicing elements of their profession
for as long as they can remember. They have taken piano lessons, voice
lessons, or played some other instrument since they were a child. They
have had more formal training than a medical doctor or an astronaut. You
have only to count the hours put into their craft from the time they
first two-stepped onto this planet to realize that theirs is more a lifestyle
than a profession. They have spent their lives developing their abilities
as musicians.

Most music teachers that I know are at one time or another struck with
the "Sunday Night Syndrome." Some as early as Wednesday! More relevant

perhaps, is that important moment when they had to decide how they were going to spend the practical portion of their lives as artists. Undoubtedly, they have at one moment, or perhaps annually, had to answer the profound question of their lives, "What on Earth am I going to do with these talents and all of this training?"

Most music teachers that I know had several legitimate choices. They could have become a professional performer, a recording artist, conductor, composer, or chosen any number of related professions. Or, if they also were blessed with the gift of communication skills, a love for the process as much as the result, and a desire to help shape the future of humanity, they could become a teacher.

> *There is no better way
> to spend your life
> than as a music teacher.*

"It is our choices that show what we really are, far more than our abilities." Think about it again this year and I think you'll find the evidence is pretty compelling. Want to make sure that your contribution to the world grows with each accomplishment? Be an artist. Your art will out live you. Want to make sure that the value you put in giving, sharing, and nurturing makes a difference in the world for now and forever? Become a teacher. Your lessons will outlive you. Want it all? Be a teacher of music. Your abilities will outlive you.

In the end we all share the same planet, enjoy the warmth of the same sun, the shimmer of the same moon. And, we all share the responsibility of contributing to this planet and the others with whom we share it. There is no better way to spend your life than as a music teacher. With the indisputable ability of music to nurture, inspire, motivate and heal, use your abilities to be the best music teacher you have trained so long to be. Your song will outlive you.

So we begin a new school year with new songs, new goals, new students, new dreams, and hopefully a renewed commitment to lose ourselves in the joy of our music and the art of teaching it. It may not be the easy choice, but it's the right one.

The Invitation

Come walk with me!
Where the grass is kissed by the April mist or the morning dew
And walk with me under mistletoe in November snow
when the day is new
Hand in hand we can glide through this world side by side
With a friend we can give it a chance
Walk with me and I know that wherever we go
There'll be joy and if you'd like we'll dance!

Oh dance with me!
While the music plays and the couples sway under winking stars
Come dance with me as the planets spin
and the world we're in is completely ours
Arm in arm, heart to heart nothing moves us apart
As we waltz through this life just like one
Dance with me and I know that wherever we go,
There'll be love and if you'd like we'll run!

Yes run with me!
Through the fields of grain in the pouring rain or the midday sun
Come run with me when the air is clear and the moon feels near
and the world is one
And we won't look behind and we won't feel regret
for the things that we didn't even try
Run with me and you'll find that the world can be kind
There'll be joy, there'll be love, we'll be free and if you'd like we'll fly!

Come walk with me! Oh! Dance with me!
Yes! Run with me! Come on … Let's fly!

TEACHER
APPRECIATION WEEK

Have you heard the one about the old man who, while standing near the edge of a high cliff, encourages a younger man to come and have a closer look over the abyss?

"Come over here and have a better look," he suggests.

"I don't know," replies the young man cautiously, "it seems awfully risky and I have a lot of life ahead of me."

"No really, come and have a look," prods the old-timer, "it's really quite exciting!"

"I don't know. I'm not very brave and what should happen if I fall?"

"Get over here and look over this cliff!" demands the old man, forcefully enough that the younger fellow acquiesces and treads gingerly to the edge of the cliff. Sure enough, just as he reaches the spot where he could not go another step without falling, the old man places a hand on the small of his back and gives him a hearty shove. And the young man flies.

In May we celebrate Teacher Appreciation Week. What a fine idea! These great, unsung heroes of our time finally get an entire week to be showered with gestures and words of well-deserved gratitude. You probably won't get a huge bonus, but in the words of Mrs. Loman in *Death of a Salesman*, to you "attention must be paid" at least for a week.

Like the young man in the story, each of us probably had a teacher who at a crucial time encouraged us to take the necessary risks that caused us to do things we never dreamed we could. Like him, each of us had someone who put their hand in the small of our back (or perhaps it was their foot in the seat of our pants), and gave us the opportunity to overcome our own fears and self-doubt, enabling us to soar. Similarly, throughout history most great figures have been greatly influenced by one, or many teachers who played vital roles at impressionable times in their lives. Helen Keller had Anne Sullivan, Aristotle had Plato, Mowgli had Balloo. This is the week we say thanks to all of them. This is the week we say thanks to all of you who play that invaluable role in the lives of students every single day.

Speaking of soaring, in May we also pay tribute to Charles Lindbergh, who in 1927 made his record setting flight aboard the *Spirit Of St. Louis*, from New York to Paris. There are those who find Charles Lindbergh a man of considerable controversy in American history. He certainly led a colorful life in and out of the spotlight. But he is an American hero for the indisputable courage he demonstrated not only during those 33½ hours in the air on that historic flight, but throughout a lifetime of taking risks and advancing the quality of every future American's life. Flying across the country or across the ocean is something we take for granted in our world. Thousands of people do it every single day. But heroes are often those who did it first. Charles Lindbergh led the way.

Do you ever look at your classroom of students and wonder which of them might become an American hero of the stature of Charles Lindbergh? Do you suppose his own teachers in Little Falls, Minnesota where he grew up recognized his heroic possibilities even at a very young age? Sometimes larger than life potential is obvious very early on. But in other instances, latent heroic possibility can be very hard to recognize and may not shine through until just the right circumstances present themselves. Would the teacher in a one-room schoolhouse in Illinois really imagine that a boy

It is our job to maintain a classroom that encourages risk-taking in a safe and friendly environment.

named Abraham Lincoln would someday be among the greatest presidents of the United States of America? Did Anne Sullivan really think that multiple-challenged Helen Keller would grow up to be one of the most inspiring and significant figures of our nation's entire history?

One of the best things about being a music teacher is that at one time or another you probably have contact with every single student in the school. (I know what you're thinking. There are a few with whom you might like a little less contact!) But sooner or later, for better or worse, eventually you've had them all. In some of them you will definitely witness extraordinary potential demonstrated in quick minds, academic ability, sharp wit, innate musical talent, or other "better than average" attributes. In others, a heroic attribute may be much harder to discern. But, you know what? It's there. It's always there. As teachers it's our responsibility and our joy to keep pushing forward so that when the opportunity arises, potential, heroic or modest, has a chance to be realized. As teachers, it is our job to maintain a classroom that encourages risk-taking in a safe and friendly environment, a place where it is safe to succeed and equally safe to fail, a place where potential is in a petri dish and can't help but grow.

It's not enough to latch on to the select few that seem to "get it" right away. As a teacher it's our job to nurture, discipline, encourage, and embolden all of them. Who are we to decide which of them might someday change the world? Our job is to help them be the kind of people who want to change it for the better. Like my friend composer Mac Huff always says, "as teachers it is our job to help arrange success."

There are heroes in your classroom. You can bet on it. You are one of them. You are one of them when you make your classroom a safe place for your students to take risks and sometimes fly. You are one of them when you look for the hidden potential in even the most troubling child and don't give up on them no matter what the circumstances. You are one of them when you teach every child that they have *a place in your choir*. For a week in May we will treat you like a hero and call it Teacher Appreciation Week. But for what you do week in and week out as you nurture all of the future Albert Einsteins, Jesse Owens, Booker T. Washingtons, Nellie Blys and Charles Lindberghs you will truly be a hero all year long.

My Teacher
With Alan Billingsley

That's my teacher, my favorite teacher,
Smart and good and true.
Ev'ry creature should meet my teacher
Friend to me and you.

She taught me all my A B C's,
And even got me through X Y Z!
In writing she was in control
In reading she was on a roll!
She does her best to educate,
Yes my teacher is really great!

Arithmetic was not so bad.
In math, I learned that I could add.
She made me feel like I could count
And come up with the right amount.
I almost love geometry,
Yes, my teacher is there for me!

In soccer she can really score.
In kickball she can burn the floor.
She makes me run a country mile.
But when I'm down she makes me smile.
I only wish she'd take a rest
But my teacher sure is the best.

My teacher, my teacher,
Making learning fun.
My teacher, my teacher,
My teacher is number one!

WE GIVE THEE THANKS

"But why do I have to be the Turkey?" wailed a fourth grader by the name of Tommy Ostinato. "Because none of the other boys will do it, and you're my son and maybe if you do it, so will some of the others. Besides, you'll look cute as a button with this little gobble around your chin and I know I can count on you to handle the solo in 'Shall We Gather At the River,'" answered Mrs. Ostinato in one well-supported breath. She was, of course, Tommy Ostinato's mother, and not coincidently the elementary music teacher at PS 134. She said all of this as she pinned the fan of multi-colored construction paper tail feathers on her reluctant portrayer of poultry.

"But, Mom!"

"No arguing. You're not named Tom for nothing. I need you to do this. You'll be the hit of the pageant."

"It's not dignified!"

"Not dignified? How can you say that? Benjamin Franklin wanted the turkey to be our national bird he thought it so grand and proud."

"But, Mom!"

"Besides, you're a fourth grader. I'll worry about your dignity."

Tommy knew it was useless trying to reason with her. Once the week before a show hit, all reason was cast aside. When Mrs. Ostinato (a.k.a. Mommy) set her sights on the final performance, one may as well acquiesce and practice gobbling. Besides, being a turkey isn't as bad as playing the little bunny in the spring show, which he had to do in third grade, the curly-toed leprechaun in the Saint Patrick's Day program, that was second grade material, and worst of all, the littlest angel in the Christmas pageant, hung by a cable for a full forty-five minutes without a potty break. Tommy almost wished he was a preacher's kid or maybe even had a parent in administration. There was definitely some burden that came with being the son of the elementary school music teacher. In the end, Tommy knew that a kid had to do what a kid had to do, and what this kid had to do was be the turkey in the Thanksgiving Day program, for Mrs. Ostinato, his mom's sake.

Tommy was not embarrassed by his mother like some of the other children seemed to be. In fact, he was proud of how hard she worked to make every child and every member of the faculty and even community feel as though they were an important part of the choir. He knew she was diligent in her efforts to teach in often impossible circumstances. When it came to scheduling she was a genius both at home and at school. She knew all the children's names and a whole lot about them. She took on extra tasks that no one else would tackle. When someone needed music for a Remembrance Day program, Tommy's mom was there. When entertainment was requested to lighten up a contentious school board meeting, it was Tommy's mommy who filled the bill. When class sizes for classroom teachers grew by ten percent, they doubled her load giving her often fifty or even sixty children at a time, with no aide! And she did it! True, embarrassment was close when Mrs. Ostinato went to a summer music workshop and returned home with the announcement that she had mastered the "cabbage patch" move, the "smurf" and several new, rad, hip hop maneuvers. "You are not going to demonstrate those to the class are you?" Tommy asked in horror. "I most certainly am!" responded Mrs. Ostinato with utter confidence. The next day she did, and the class loved it. And the class loved her. And Tommy did too.

*Once the week before a show hit,
all reason was cast aside.*

So, what's the use and what's the big deal? If the music teacher happens to be your mom and it's Thanksgiving, you might as well strap on a few tail feathers and a gobble and prance around the stage as though this kind of thing is normal. It's going to happen whether you like it or not. And she's worth the risk. You see Tommy's intentions were noble indeed. They really were.

Unfortunately, as fate would have it, the fourth grade class at PS 134 had recently been plagued with several cases of the 24-hour flu. The epidemic seemed to be growing like a blue-ribboned butternut squash in late summer. There was nothing anyone could do about it but try to hold on and regularly call for a janitor. Its timing was remarkable and finally caught up with, you guessed it, noble Tommy Ostinato not more than ninety minutes before the big Thanksgiving Day extravaganza.

"Sorry Mom. I just don't think I can …" Tommy's apology was cut short as he raced down the hall and "made it." He was sent home with a neighbor lady, his turkey feathers dragging. Mrs. Ostinato went into emergency mode.

The audience filed in. Parents had taken off from work. The administration was there as were important dignitaries from the school board and the townsfolk. Cell phones were turned off. Well, most of them. The house lights dimmed in the "No-Purpose Room." On with the show.

The second grade Native Americans were resplendent. Their costumes were authentic down to the last detail. (Well, that's not exactly true. If one looked closely one could easily see the waistband and leggings of Jimmy Sissolo's Sponge Bob Square Pants boxer shorts underneath his faux leather loincloth.) But moccasins and face paint were running everywhere and the treble tribal "whoops!" were fiercely adorable over the sound of the coffee can drum.

The pilgrims entered next. Stovepipe hats, white paper collars and genuine buckles on their boots made the third graders look as pious as Puritans. "We give Thee thanks!" they chanted over and over. "We give Thee thanks."

Even the animals of the farm and forest had important roles to play. The first graders were a hit as deer, bear, badgers, and bunnies. There was even a groundhog, since Melissa Gunderson's mother had made such an adorable costume for the February program and it still fit in most places.

All were in their places and everyone was fully aware that the only character not on stage yet was the star of any Thanksgiving Day pageant, the turkey. "We're proud to share our bounty with you," Miles Standish announced. "Our corn, our rice, our tender beef jerky. If that's not enough, take a look at this prize, the main event, our favorite Tom turkey."

At this point of course, everyone knew that the turkey was supposed to enter gobbling to the oohs, aahs, and applause of his appreciative audience. But Tommy Ostinato was home sick with the flu. What would happen? No one quite knew.

Yet, right on cue from stage left strutted a turkey, gobbling proudly and shaking his tail feathers for all he was worth. Granted he was about six-foot-two and sported at least a five o'clock shadow beneath his wobbling gobble. Who could it be? Well, everyone knew.

"Isn't that the fellow who always plays Santa Claus in the holiday show?" one mother whispered to another.

"Yes! I believe it is."

"And I know I've seen him as Rudolph on more than one occasion, not to mention Father Time, the Easter Bunny, Abraham Lincoln, and once even the Little Old Lady From Pasadena."

"I know that guy! He's always carrying in sound equipment, setting up risers, providing treats for after the show, driving the bus to the nursing home performances, copying rehearsal CDs, building sets or running the lights for the show. What do you know? Now he's the turkey!"

"Of course! Of course!" you could hear the whispers, "Of course it is! That turkey is Mr. Ostinato!"

And so it was. And so he always did, because in the end Tommy, the only thing more challenging than being the music teacher's son is being the music teacher's spouse.

So, a Thanksgiving toast to each and every one of them. Those who schlep and cart, video and mix, encourage and applaud, strut and yes, sometimes even gobble. May they all forgive us some quiet day. For now, indeed, we give thee thanks.

All the People Said Thanks!
With Emily Crocker

Shadows lift, morning breaks, warmed by autumn sun,
Just like a thousand years ago, a new day has begun!
Earth and sea, sun and moon, wonders small and grand,
Fill our horn of plenty with the bounty of the land!

All the people said thanks.
All the people said thanks.
Hand in hand by the river banks
All the people said thanks.

The people looked around their world with amazement and awe.
They bowed their heads with gratitude for all the gifts they saw.
Come ye thankful people come, all is gathered in.
Sing your song of harvest home and let the feast begin!

All the people said thanks.
All the people said thanks.
Hand in hand by the river banks
All the people said thanks.

SURVIVING DECEMBER

It must be the fact that it's ninety-eight degrees in California today that I decided to concentrate on a special holiday message to all of my musical friends. It started, quite cleverly I thought, with a rewording of the classic Clement C. Moore poem, "A Visit From Saint Nicholas" with verses that reflected upon the dizzying predicament faced by most music teachers during that last month leading up to the holidays. There are concerts, teas, caroling parties, and open houses, all of which demand " a little live music from that wonderful music program up at the school." Not such an original idea I admit, but hey, its ninety-eight degrees! Unfortunately, the first line of my hopeful, holiday missive came out:

> 'Twas the night before Christmas and in front of the choir
> The teacher was thinking, "When can I retire?"

And it went downhill from there.

As a music teacher/Holiday Extravaganza producer, the December goal of many a music teacher seems to be to survive it! By the time most of us have recovered it's mid-January and we're starting to think about President's Day programs, spring assessments, and the educational worthiness of the Easter Bunny Hop. We are hardly allowed to enjoy the holiday spirit in our own right, as we are so busy making everyone else's season bright.

Yet, it does seem that the winter holidays are a good time to reflect upon all of the lives you impact when you make room for all of the students in your music program; not only making room, but making each feel valued for the unique backgrounds and qualities they bring to the festive gathering. Perhaps there is no more obvious time during the year when we are encouraged, in fact expected, to cover all of our bases, and include everybody in our musical endeavors. No matter where you live and teach in this land you are expected to musically celebrate Hanukkah, La Posadas, Kwanzaa, Ramadan, and the myriad of other special occasions recognized by the variety of people who make up our shrinking world. This is a very good thing!

As challenging as it may seem at times, aren't we lucky to be surrounded by the magnificent kaleidoscope of humanity that makes our land both colorful and challenging? Children need to learn respect for those who are different than they are; who celebrate different beliefs and customs; whose traditions, although different, are as deeply rooted and sacred as their own. In this century children everywhere, Jewish or not, know the story of the Macaques and the miracle of the lights celebrated through Hanukkah. Children everywhere can recite the seven virtues that are recognized in the African American Kwanzaa celebration. And, children everywhere, be they Christian or not, know the story of a baby born in a manger who many believe is the Savior of humankind. And they learned it best in music class. Yes, indeed I think it's true! The lessons you learn by memorizing a story song, or a melody or a dance from another person's history are lessons you will never forget. They become a part of the fabric of who you are. They become a part of you. This is a very good thing!

The lessons you learn by memorizing a story song, or a melody or a dance from another person's history are lessons you will never forget.

We all recognize the challenges that result from the opinions of the adults around us, though children rarely have these concerns. Can we say the word Christmas? Can Santa show up? Is there a higher percentage of one traditions' music being represented than another? Are we proselytizing? Are we making someone feel left out or different? Shall we just skip the whole thing? I don't think so.

As simplistic as it may sound, a thick skin, a reasonable administrative hierarchy, and a balanced approach to celebrating the vast holiday traditions of our country seems to me the most fair, reasonable, and safest approach to keeping all of these wonderful traditions alive. By treating each of the various holidays with honor and respect we learn more about each other, we truly celebrate our likenesses and our differences, and we remind every child in our lives that they have *a place in the choir*!

Finally, I have a poem to share from the bottom of my heart. Unlike my attempt at parody, my father was in my estimation, a gifted poet as well as a loving parent, masterful teacher and pretty durn good singer behind the wheel of the Chevrolet. He loved to read poetry, listen to poetry, and even write a few verses himself. Here's one he wrote so many years ago. A holiday gift to us I'd like to share with you.

A Christmas Wish to You

By Donald Jacobson (1929–1999)

May you be blessed once again
With the ability to view Christmas
As a child views Christmas;
With eyes filled with wonder
And hearts and minds filled
With faith, hope and love.
For all the world should be a child
At Christmas Time.

And may you once again capture
The spirit of the season:
The spirit which makes giving
More enjoyable than receiving and
replaces greed with generosity and humility.
The spirit which causes the "Golden Rule"
To be accepted practice for a time.
For all the world should have the Christmas Spirit
At Christmas Time.

And may the New Year bring to you
A continuation of the feelings that prevail
At Christmas Time. The feelings of goodness
And neighborly concern and the
Worthiness of man. The feeling too that
Somehow beyond this special season
"Goodwill to fellow man" might still prevail.
For all the world should have that Christmas feeling
At Christmas Time.

May you know the beauty of this season
And may that beauty last throughout the year.
Not only the beauty of the greens, but better
Still, the inner glow that seems to
Surface best at this time of year.
Things that seem commonplace at
Other times acquire specialness at Christmas.
All the world should know the source
And meaning of the beauty that is seen
At Christmas Time.

THE THING
WITH FEATHERS

A teacher told me this great story one day and for the life of me I can't remember her name. I hope she'll forgive me and make herself known to me again someday. I'll just call her Mrs. T. I'll call the kid Joey Stendahl because that was the name of the kid who terrorized me for several years long ago. I'm kidding. Sort of.

Joey Stendahl was the rascally-est kid in the whole class. He had some challenges, including disorders whose acronyms I sometimes find difficult to understand. He could be a distraction to everybody around him. He could be downright mean. He acted like he hated everyone and everything. Joey was at times difficult to love, even for Mrs. T, who absolutely loved everybody. "Joey, sit down now." "Joey quit bothering, Jessica." Joey get away from that window." "Joey put down that mallet." "Joey! Joey! Joooeeeeey!" Joey Stendahl was the rascally-est kid in the whole class.

For months, Mrs. T the music teacher, and all of the other faculty members worked on Joey's behavior. They all agreed, well they all "hoped," that if they could just get Joey to behave with respect and act as though he cared about the people around him, maybe some of those actions would become habit and Joey might make a positive contribution to society ... or at least not disrupt it completely for everyone else on the planet. However, nothing seemed to work. Oh, Joey made tiny little steps forward here and there, but for the most part he was still a terror with which to be reckoned.

Then one day word came down that Joey and his parents were going to be leaving town, moving to another state for career opportunities. Restraining the honest, but guilt-ridden relief in the pits of their stomachs, the teachers, including Mrs. T, decided to do something special for Joey before he left. They put together a little slide show of some of the things that Joey had participated in at school, editing out the mug shots and unsanctioned food fights he instigated. Some of the students got involved too and wrote little going away poems for Joey and drew pictures for him on farewell cards. Joey actually paid attention all day long and seemed to be genuinely moved by the display of his friends and teachers. Near the end of this very special day Joey actually walked up and sat down next to Mrs. T. He even laid his scruffy head against her shoulder in a quiet mood almost unrecognizable to all. Mrs. T could not resist. "Well Joey," she said softly. "It seems that all of the events of the day meant a lot to you. I thought I maybe even saw you tear up a little. Could it be that you're feeling sad about leaving all of us behind?"

"Well, Mrs. T" Joey started, "the truth is that about fifty percent of that came from the fact that I knew you people would want me to act like that and I thought, it's one day, what the heck." Mrs. T felt sad and deflated. Then Joey went on, actually taking Mrs. T's hand and placing it on his own heart, "the rest of it Mrs. T came from here."

The older I get the less I am absolutely sure of. I fully expect to die with a completely blank upstairs. Some might suggest that it appears there's not long left. Hmm. But there are a few things of which I am actually quite confident. They are things I believe.

> *A word of warning; I am one of those people who believe that a belief is a belief is a belief and that just because I believe it, does not necessarily make it so. It's a belief! Someone else might believe something else. Their belief is just as valid as mine. Yes! Really! You better believe it!*

Now, for those of you who chose to continue, let me say that I am positive that "All God's children got *a place in the choir*." I think that someday this will perhaps be my last coherent thought before I join that great gospel choir in the sky, which I fully expect is co-conducted by Moses Hogan and Fred Bock. It might very well be the most consistently reinforced of all of my beliefs. I believe that every goofy, clunky, obnoxious, shy, overbearing, spoiled, deprived, sweet, sour, loud, soft, harsh, tender child belongs. I believe it is my job, responsibility, and honor to welcome them and nurture them in their life-long quest for harmony and meaning. I choose to embrace that responsibility through music and movement. I *believe* it is a very effective venue in which to help children become beautiful human beings. Even Joey Stendahl.

Yesterday I told a fib. Well, not exactly a fib, well, you decide. I had a deadline for a writing assignment and I told my publisher that I had an important meeting in the afternoon that would prevent me from meeting that deadline. I went skiing with Roger Emerson. I couldn't help it! The sky was so blue, the snow so fresh. The mountain was like a magnet. It was Roger's fault! Please don't tell my publisher. I *believe* that I made the right choice. (See asterisk above regarding beliefs.) Michael Mertens went too. Maybe it was *his* fault. Yes, I believe it was.

The best part about skiing with Michael and Roger is the slow ride up the chair lift. The best conversations in the world happen there, in mid-air, minutes before you throw all sense of logic and grace out the window and hurl yourself totally out of control down the ridiculously steep face of a fourteen-thousand-foot mountain. We always talk of politics or matters of faith, how many music stands eighty-seven billion dollars could buy, what on earth were those Super Bowl halftime performers thinking about, and on and on. Yesterday was one of the best conversations of all. We talked about life and death and the extraordinary variety of people and events that make each day both routine and unique. Dan and Mark are both at funerals today for their beloved mothers. Janet just told us she's going to have a second baby. The editorial staff at Hal Leonard is all working overtime in order to get everything ready for another publishing season. Roger's daughter is visiting colleges looking to begin a new stage in her life. My brother Kevin is jetting off to Turkey to film a video for the Lutheran Church, brother Kerry is off on a Fulbright to the Czech Republic. People are working, children are playing, daddies are singing lullabies, and mommies are fixing leaking faucets. My deadline is passing and I'm going skiing. Stuff like this goes on everyday. I know what you're thinking, "John, stuff like that's been going on for forty-thousand years. This is not that remarkable." I believe it is. It keeps me going. I believe in hope. Here is one of my all time favorite verses.

> *Hope is the thing with feathers*
> *That perches in the soul*
> *And sings the tune without the words*
> *And never stops, at all.*
> Emily Dickinson

The end of another school year is a great time to re-evaluate our own lives and the contributions we make to the lives of others. A teacher's year often ends with either a bang or a whimper. If you've taught for enough years you probably realize despite your best efforts, that's the way it is. You win some, and you lose some. But you never give up the belief that there is hope that every child who has come in contact with you might just make it once they leave your care. You have also come to realize that although there are easier ways to make a living, you care about the future. And you have come to believe that there is no better way to brighten the future than by investing in those who will live in it, even Joey Stendahl.

Hope lives. The world is a remarkable place every single day and Joey Stendahl deserves *a place in the choir*. I believe this.

The Most Beautiful Kid in the World

With Alan Billingsley

The most beautiful kid in the world
Is here with me today.
The most beautiful kid in the world
Came by my house to play.
No matter what you do.
This much I know is true.
The most beautiful kid in the world is you!

It doesn't really matter if you're big or if you're small.
I only hope you understand that you're the best of all to me.
The most beautiful kid in the world is here with me today.
The most beautiful kid in the world,
Came by my house to play.
And no matter what you do,
This much I know is true.

The most beautiful kid in the world,
The most beautiful kid in the world,
The most beautiful child
In the most beautiful kid in the world is you!
Is you!
It's you!

ANYONE CAN SING

"Wouldn't the woods be silent if only the best birds sang."

Shari Lewis (a hero of mine, remember Lamb Chop?) gave her mother credit for that brilliant little saying. I'm not sure if she was the first to say it or not, but it's a keeper in my book.

Anyone can sing. (Pause) You can teach anyone to sing. (Grand pause) Okay, anyone can play the recorder. (Groan) You can teach anyone to play recorder. (Big loud groan) Okay, anyone can play the xylophone to some degree. (Wince) Okay, if you take off all of the right notes, anyone can make music on a xylophone. (Cautious nod) Okay, anyone can hold a flag. (Smile)

I spent the first two summers of my professional career as a performer holding a spear in the background of a medley from the musical *Jesus Christ Superstar*. It was about all I could handle. My hosannas were resounding! The next year I held a flag for the patriotic show. Anyone can hold a flag. And yes. You *can* teach anyone to sing.

Here we are heading into another year of teaching music; maybe the first, maybe the last, maybe one of many behind us and many yet to come. How does it feel? My friend Stew who teaches middle school orchestra says that when he conducts a four beat pattern he sometimes finds himself thinking, "(1) same, (2) darn, (3) thing, (4) again! (1) Same, (2) darn, (3) thing, (4) again!" (I always thought it was (1) floor, (2) wall, (3) wall, (4) ceiling, but that's another story.) Heading back into the classroom after summer vacation or even a nice long weekend can sometimes bring to mind "same, darn, thing, again!" (Knowing Stew, I will tell you that I think that by the end of some long days of teaching he changes beat two to something stronger but generally keeps it to himself!)

So, here we go again. Some years it is easier than others to head back to school. Some years it's almost impossible to get revved up for it. But we do it, because we understand the value of helping a child find their voice in a world that tries hard to drown them out. We do it because we know the value of music in a child's life and because in the words of that sagacious philosopher Nicole Kidman, "art is important." We do it because we know that anyone can sing. (Pause) Okay, we can teach anyone to sing. (Grand pause) Okay, anyone can hold a flag. (Smile)

All kidding aside, I think that most of us do feel that we can get anyone to make music at some level. It may not be what we consider beautiful singing or playing, but we can move them along, along with a song.

Those who would teach music or any of the arts have an awesome opportunity before them, not only to teach our wards to sing but also to feel. The challenge is not only to lead them to play but to experience. Not just to hear, but to listen. Not just to look, but to see.

I believe that when you teach music the easiest part is to pass along the knowledge of notes and melody, harmony and tone production. It's relatively simple to teach history and performance, structure and form. But can we also teach our students to feel? Can we also teach them a joy for learning, enthusiasm for life and art? Can we teach them to have a passion for compassion? Can we teach them to love? Can we teach them what it is to be human? I believe we can.

Most of us who teach music have become quite adept at teaching the performance of music. Learning to perform is worthy and legitimate at so many levels. We can use the same tools and skills we possess to help our young students get beyond the presentation of music and into the experience of it. When a young person is led to discover the thrill of a beautiful melody, the turn of a phrase or an exhilarating cadence, they experience music in an entirely different way on an entirely different plane even if the applause may only be their own. This brush with beauty can be life altering. They are listening, not just hearing. They are seeing, not just looking.

Anyone can sing! Yes they can. You *can* teach anyone to sing. But, more importantly you can use your own experience in music to help children learn to love, to feel joy, to know pathos and exhilaration, passion and compassion, and in the end, to be more human.

You really just never know how your own enthusiasm for your art is going to affect some child. A cruddy french horn player performs in a marching band that plays "Send In The Clowns" on the football field for homecoming (I'm not kidding, it happened!), and becomes an accomplished performer of the sophisticated music of Stephen Sondheim. Another young person is blown away by your demonstrated devotion to Edna St. Vincent Millay and in their own times of anguish and despair is comforted by, "The soul can split the sky in two, and let the love of God shine through." A child can sing and play, listen and hear, look and see, present and experience. You can give that to them perhaps more effectively than anyone in their lives, for you teach. And better yet, you teach music. (Pause, groan, smile)

Now that's something to hold a spear and wave a flag over.

Can't Help Singing

With Mac Huff

Every time the music plays a change comes over me.
The beat will thump, my joints will jump to a joyful symphony.
When I hear a melody I just lose control.
My heart will hop, my pulse will pop,
So let the good times roll!

Can't help singing, can't help singing
Listen to the music play!
Can't help hummin' when the drummer's drumming
I just get carried away.
Music's got ahold of my heart, music's got me movin' along.
With the joy it's bringing, I can't help singing my song!

I snap my fingers and tap my feet to the swingin' sound of jazz.
My heart will skip, my brain will flip with all this razz-ma-tazz.
You can't stop this feeling, you might as well let go.
The sound will shock, the house will rock,
Sing out and join the show!

Can't help singing, can't help singing
Listen to the music play!
Can't help hummin' when the drummer's drumming
I just get carried away.
Music's got ahold of my heart, music's got me movin' along.
With the joy it's bringing, I can't help singing my song!

THIS IS MY SONG

When I was fifteen years old I auditioned for and was selected to perform in a group we had in my state called The Kids From Wisconsin. I grew up in Wisconsin in case you didn't make that connection. "The Kids" were sort of an All-State Show Choir made up of about twenty-four singer/dancers and a twelve-piece band. It was produced by a retired Lieutenant Colonel of the Air Force by the name of Mark Azzolina and costumed by his elegant wife, Betty. Kurt Chalgren musically directed it with arrangements by Nick Nichols, affectionately known as "Uncle Nick." Uncle Nick was the Colonel's brother and used to do arrangements for the Jackie Gleason Show among other things. Our band of singers was choreographed by the extremely creative Tom Terrien, a man I give tons of credit for teaching me how to be a performer and alas, a choreographer. If I have a style at all, it is mostly an imitation of Mr. Terrien and a few other remarkable teachers I worked under in the ensuing years. Mr. Terrien had a big sheepdog named George who traveled on the bus with us like a mascot. The experience was absolutely life changing for me and continues to be for young and extroverted Cheese Heads even as we speak. I learned so much when I started performing as a "Kid." Oh my goodness, I learned so much!

First of all, I was *by far* the least experienced singer/dancer of the cast. I mean I was terrible. So no one was more shocked than I when offered the job a few weeks after my flailing and howling audition. I couldn't march, so I certainly couldn't soft-shoe. When I Lindy-ed, Uncle Nick could not contain his laughter. Tom Terrien was nearly in tears, but not the laughing kind. My vocal training consisted mostly of trying to be heard over the other eleven voices in the family station wagon. (Remember, I'm one of ten kids, each with a healthy set of lungs and a feisty competitive spirit, even if the competition is simply who can remember the most verses for "Beautiful Savior" or "Are You Going To Scarborough Fair?") During my first year as a member The Kids From Wisconsin we performed a medley of songs from the Webber and Rice rock musical *Jesus Christ Superstar*. Consequently, all of the really hot singers and dancers like Roxy Meggars and Dennis Kotecki were strategically placed downstage front and center, dancing as though they were right out of the Broadway cast, and those of us who marched like gorillas stood in the back and held spears! The second season we did a patriotic medley. Roxy and Dennis tap-danced. I held a flag. Still, I looked smart and smashing in Betty Azzolina's red, polyester Eisenhower jacket, blue polyester pants, and white polyester (do you notice a theme here?) polo shirt with red, white, and blue ribbing; two buttons buttoned, never three, no, never three.

> *It is here that my notion was affirmed that everybody on Earth has a song inside of them, and every song is as legitimate as the next.*

Another time I will regale you with my remarkable progress and the fact that I am proof that one is never too old to learn, that good teaching can make a silk purse from a sow's ear (although I never understood why one would want to), or that song and dance can emanate from two left feet, a determined spirit, and remarkable teachers. Instead I want to tell you about the single most important lesson I learned in the three summers I spent as a Kid From Wisconsin. As we traveled around from county fair to county fair, Cheese Festivals to Corn Fests, Pickle Days to Dairy Nights, I learned a lesson that I pray every day I am able to stay true to. It was here that I became an adult. It is here that my notion was affirmed that everybody on Earth has a song inside them, and every song is as legitimate as the next. It was here that I confirmed that what my father and mother, grandparents and kinfolk, teachers and influential adults had been telling me was ever so true; all God's children got *a place in the choir!*

You see, even in a state like Wisconsin, which way back then might have seemed remarkably homogenous to people from more diverse parts of the country, the "Kids" were comprised of a mix of "types" that this li'l-old-boy-from-de-sticks found startling and incredibly exciting. Hardly anybody was just like me! Beside the fact that most of them could actually sing and dance they were all just so different from the folks in my little town of Blair,

909 people, most of who were Olsens or Jacobsons, Hansons or Stephansons. (In retrospect, I think that most of the "Kids" were pretty much just like me, searching for the song that makes them, them. It took years to recognize this.)

In the "Kids" we had a guy with the improbable name of SaLoutos! (I'm sorry, but there were no Greeks in Blair that I'm aware of!) Dave SaLoutos ended up being my college roommate after we graduated from "Kids" and then he became the ringmaster at the Ringling Brother's Circus World Museum in Baraboo, Wisconsin. He had and still has a great song in him. Chris Wozny was a Kid From Wisconsin, too. There were no Woznys in Blair I assure you! There were also Koteckis and Meggars, Schaefers and Ziebells, Granums and Delgers, Dorns and Baxters and on and on, every one of them so different and amazing to me. Each of these "Kids" had a remarkable song in them. Each of them had a great song to sing.

There was another boy named David, too. I'll just call him David B. I'll never forget him. He was a "Kid" for three years or so. During that time, all of us changed, as kids and "Kids" are wont to do. Every year David B. changed too. None of us knew what was going on with him but we didn't like the change. He went from being an extremely personable boy to a distant and irresponsible young man. He would show up late for rehearsals or not at all. He became moody and morose. He went from being our buddy to being our annoyance. In short, most of us "Kids" just wanted him to go away. We felt he was letting us down. "Send him home," we murmured. "He doesn't fit in."

Colonel Azzolina said "No, he stays." Mr. Terrien said, "He stays." Mr. Chalgren said, "He's just trying to find his song. He stays." Uncle Nick and Mrs. Azzolina said, "He's one of us! He stays." I'm pretty sure that even George woofed, "He stays!" Not one of our teachers would abandon David B. as easy as it may have seemed to all of us. They stuck with him as they stuck with all of us.

What does that mean, "He's just trying to find his song?" Having somehow miraculously made it to adulthood, I believe that every child and every adult has a song in them that with luck and nourishment will have a chance to get out. For some, it might manifest itself as a knack for computers or science. For others it might be athletics or poetry, logic or intuition, art or auto-mechanics. But it's there. And it's crying to be heard.

The teachers who made up the staff of Kids From Wisconsin recognized the critical role they played in all of our personal song searches, especially someone like David B. When all the rest of us wanted to abandon him because it would have made *our* lives easier, it would have made our teacher's lives easier too. But they said "No, he stays. He stays." Unanimously they knew that helping David find his song was the most important role they had to play as adults. We all benefited from their sage decision. I wish I could tell you that David B. went on to become this totally well adjusted adult and lived happily ever after, despite the years of direct exposure to sweaty polyester. He may have. But we have lost touch. Yet, I know for sure his chances of doing so would have been greatly diminished had the adults who surrounded him when he was struggling as a "Kid" abandoned him. As teachers we know that children can sometimes be very, very hard on each other. It is our responsibility, and indeed our privilege, to keep an eye on those that might be left behind and support them even if they may not be the easiest to love.

I hope that every child is as lucky as this "Kid" (meaning me) was, and that every teacher and every parent recognizes as one of its primary assignments their support of a child's search to find themselves. Then, when a child, be it SaLoutos, or Kotecki, Wozny or Jacobson stands before them and declares, "This is my song," that parent or teacher will courageously respond, "You bet it is. And you go ahead and sing it." And when a child winds up in our choir who is difficult and inconsistent, obnoxious or challenging in any way, shape, or form we'll have the courage and compassion to say, "You stay. You stay. Let's find your song together."

The Best in Me
With Cristi Cary Miller

Somewhere deep inside me there played a simple song.
But only I could hear it; only I could sing along.
Then one sunny morning someone set it free,
And all the notes from deep inside came pouring out of me.

Who would believe that this song was in me?
Who could conceive that it would set me free?
All I needed was a chance, one opportunity.
A person just like you who saw the very best in me.

Oh now you hear me singing and I can hear you too.
I can hear that melody that's there inside of you.
We can share our music and bring our dreams along.
Come and we'll make harmony while singing our own song!

Who would believe that this song was in me?
Who could conceive that it would set me free?
All I needed was a chance, one opportunity.
A person just like you who saw the very best in me.

THE GREAT DEBATE

"Did not!"
　　"Did too!"
　　"Did not!"
　　"Did too!"
　　"Did"
　　"Too"
　　"Bonehead!"
　　"Wimp!"
　　"Tattletale!"
　　"Future Show Choir Guy!"
　　(Gasp) "Mo—o—om!!"

And so the great Jacobson Brother Debate circa 1965 came to a rousing, wrestling in the living room conclusion.

I really like to believe that after Abraham Lincoln and Stephen A. Douglas had their knock down, drag out fights under the tree in Tappen Wood (or some tree anyway), they met back at Ye Ol' Silver Dollar Saloon, shook hands and shared a sudsy sarsaparilla. *(Listen, the world I live in is really quite marvelous.)* It could have happened. I choose to believe it did.

In reality *(where I actually do spend a little time)*, I am often impressed with the way in which some people who disagree with one another are able to debate their sides of the story, sometimes quite heatedly. Yet, when the debate is over they behave with respect and even friendliness toward one another. It really does happen. As one who is a bit of a political junkie, I see it all the time with members of Congress or even campaigning candidates for a particular position in the government. I marvel at it. I really do. They meet in front of their colleagues or constituents, argue their points with passion and something that passes as reason to them, and when it's over, move on with respect for their opponent's thoughtfulness, preparedness and honor. At least the good ones do. I am also one of those people who believe that most of our public servants are genuinely excellent people, with high standards and a sense of calling to serve their fellow citizens. (Really, see above about the marvelous world I live in.)

Today on the news I saw that one party in the U.S. Congress had insisted to the others that they all go into closed session to argue a point they felt needed to be made out of the eyes and ears of the television cameras and general spectators. Boy! I would have loved to hear those debates. Afterwards was the usual bluster by both party's leaders in front of the reporters for the benefit of the folks back home. But in truth, I know that a lot of these men and women from either side of the arguments that went on behind those closed doors and the ensuing press conferences, shake hands and go out for a sudsy sarsaparilla once the day is over, filled with genuine respect for the other as debater, as public servant and as human being. Well, the good ones do.

Debating, even arguing if you will, is beneficial and healthy for all if it is pursued with dignity and respect from both sides. Ears as well as mouths and hearts must be open and willing to hear the other point of view and give it true consideration. This has been a vehicle for enlightenment, well, since the Enlightenment.

How do we teach this to young people? The same way we teach a lot of things, by example. (I have to add a little footnote here in the form of a confession that I, for one, am not very good at this. It seems that whenever I get into some passionate discussion in which I have a strong opinion I get so riled up and emotional that it takes me a while to "get over it." I'm working on it. But that "future show choir guy" thing was uncalled for.)

There are fortunately, in our midst and throughout our history, people who were very good at it. Because of their level-headedness mixed with intellect, passion and respect for others, they made the world better by debating, both talking and listening. They did this while acting in a respectful manner toward all once the debate was over. I'm thinking of people like Lincoln and Douglas, Thomas Paine, Thomas Jefferson, Gandhi, Benjamin Franklin, Socrates and on and on. (I'd name some more modern ones I admire but I don't want to get in a debate over it.) These individuals were all fine debaters. None of them were right all of the time, none of them were wrong all of the time. But they listened as well as spoke and made the world better by both efforts.

As music teachers we are often put into a position in which we have to debate. We are forced to defend our position on a choice of music, a method of teaching, a justification for our very existence, why we should be given a budget, a classroom, even why Rudolph has a place in the Christmas choir. We find ourselves debating artistic as well as practical day-to-day matters. It can be very frustrating and we don't always win. However, I think that if we all took a good look at the example the great debaters in our history set for us, they would all have certain attributes that could be very helpful in our own challenges.

First of all, they were all very well prepared. They knew their stuff and were armed with facts and examples that supported their point of view. It is not enough to simply "know it in your heart" that music is good for children. You need to be able to provide concrete facts that back you up. They are out there. The good debaters remain rational even when they are emotional about their subject manner. They treat their opponents with respect, and when the debate is over, they get over it and get on with it, just as we must as teachers of music. Even if we don't get all of the support we feel we need, or win every point of the debate, we keep "making it work" because we know how very important it is.

In almost all of the great debates there is at some point common ground; some area that all can agree on even if it is very broad and the paths to get there are as divergent as east and west. Yes, believe it or not, there are certain things that most humans agree upon. Universal truths. Children deserve to be protected. Everyone deserves enough to eat. Peace on Earth is a worthy goal. So perhaps the most constructive debates will be those that begin with what we agree on as opposed to where we differ. Then the debate becomes a discussion about how to get there. There, to the same place.

This is what the tree in Tappen Wood saw, debaters finding common ground; in this case, a yearning for peace. If we all agree that something such as this is a common goal then the discussion can move forward to how we can best achieve that common goal. There will be much ranting and raving, opining and declamation. Tempers will flare. Feelings might even get hurt. But children will be watching. So let's make sure that when the debate on world peace or whether or not Rudolph has a place in the Christmas choir is over, we all shake hands and meet down the street for a sudsy sarsaparilla.

"*Future show choir guy!*"

"Why, thank you!"

We Are One!
With Mac Huff

Theme song for America Sings Abroad! Berlin, Germany, 1990

Let us sing! Let us play!
Let us dare to dream a brighter day.
We Are One!

Here we are now standing hand in hand.
Diff'rent folks from many diff'rent lands.
Joining hearts together and looking for a way,
To try to help the world hear what we say.
We Are One!

From around the world the call is loud and strong
A home of peace is where we all belong.
Wherever two are gathered a friendship has begun.
Knowing two together become one.
We Are One!

We Are One! We Are One!
Tell the world a new day has begun.
Like the rising sun, We Are One!
The world's a better place when
We Are One!

We'll face the future standing hand in hand.
Diff'rent folks from many diff'rent lands.
So raise your song together and let your voices ring.
One by one the world will start to sing. We Are One!
The world's a better place when We Are One!

DEAR JOHN

Because of the fact that I spend a lot of time in schools, churches, and parks working with children of all ages, I readily hand out my home address and e-mail to any and all. Call me crazy! I am always amazed at the things folks will tell you in a letter, especially children. I try to write back as often as I can. Here are a few of those letters from me that I hope will speak to all.

Dear Young Friends,

Let's celebrate music! For when you celebrate music, you celebrate life!

It is true that the most important moments in our lives are often best remembered by the music that accompanied them. Do you remember your last birthday? Everyone sang "Happy Birthday To You," and maybe gave you a present or two. That singing of a song on your birthday happens to children all over the world. It's one of the ways we celebrate life with music.

At the beginning of a sporting event the entire crowd stands and sings our national anthem. That happens all over the world too. Remember when you watched the medal ceremonies from the Olympics? Through the smiles and tears the champions basked in their success listening to and singing the music of their homeland. Next time you are at a sporting event or anywhere where our national anthem is sung, I hope that you will stand and sing with your whole heart. It's another one of the ways in which we use music to celebrate life.

At baseball games people link arms and sing "Take Me Out To the Ball Game." At graduation ceremonies the band plays "Pomp and Circumstance" as the graduates proudly process down the aisles, and someone sings "Climb Every Mountain" as they exit to take on the world. At weddings moms and dads and ex-boyfriends cry when someone sings "The Rose" right before the couple kisses. On the Fourth of July cannons fire as orchestras play the "1812 Overture" while fireworks light up the sky.

Music is everywhere, every day of our lives. With a little imagination some will say you can even hear music in the sound of a brook bubbling over the rocks, in the wind as it whistles through the trees, or even in the traffic as it snarls a busy street. In every case music makes it beautiful!

So come on, let's celebrate music! For when you celebrate music, you celebrate life!

Your friend,

John

Dear Young Friends,

"Be nice!" Did anybody ever say that to you? Maybe it was your mom or dad, grandmother or grandfather. Maybe it was your teacher, or maybe it was a friend. Be nice. It's only two words but I think that it is pretty good advice, don't you?

There's a saying that people sometimes say but that I personally do not believe. It says that, "Nice guys finish last." But you know what? In my long life I have never found that to be true. My experience has taught me that nice guys are always the winners. And when I say "guys" I mean "girls" too. Nice guys and nice girls always win. It just depends on how you define winning.

Being nice is not always easy. Sometimes there will be someone who comes into your life that just rubs you the wrong way. Maybe they make you feel jealous, hurt, or angry. Maybe they look, dress, or act differently than you and your friends so it's easy to make a joke about them, or talk about them behind their back. Maybe they get to do something you don't get to do, like sing a solo in the spring concert or play the quarterback while you end up at center. Maybe you think that they get all the breaks. Maybe they just haven't been very nice to you so you think, "Why should I be nice to them?"

Here's why. Nice people win. You still might not get to sing the solo and you still might have to hike the ball instead of pass it, but believe me, you win. I have met a lot of people in my life, from presidents and prime ministers to sports idols and movie stars, and I can tell you honestly that the greatest were also the nicest. They treated people with respect. They gave everybody even more than a second chance. They were kind. They were nice. That's what made them winners.

I have a challenge for all of you that I hope you will take very seriously: be nice. If there is someone getting on your nerves or bothering you, be nice. If you are feeling jealous because someone got something you didn't, be nice. If you see someone who is different and you think that making a joke about them to your friends would be fun, be nice. Be nice, and you'll be a winner every time.

Your friend,

John

P.S. What's this got to do with music? That's easy. People who make music are by far the nicest people I know!

Dear Young Friends,

What does the word "miracle" mean to you?

In my dictionary the word miracle is defined as, "an event or action that is totally amazing, extraordinary, or unexpected." In another definition a miracle is, "an event that appears to be contrary to the laws of nature." In the story "A Tree In Tappen Wood," something quite miraculous seems to happen. A small child is lost in the cold winter woods. As the blizzard grows worse and her predicament more desperate it seems that a terrible tragedy might well occur. Instead, a miracle happens. Animals of the forest, some who are the natural enemy of another, come together to protect the small child from the elements. Together they keep her warm and in the morning lead her back to safety. It's amazing! It's extraordinary! It's unexpected! It's a miracle!

From my point of view, amazing things seem to happen every single day. The moon goes down pulling the tides of the ocean along with it. The sun comes up lighting and warming the world. Plants grow and flowers bloom. Hearts beat, lungs fill with air, birds sing, children too. But these amazing things have happened so many times that by now we have all come to expect them. To be a "miracle" a thing cannot be ordinary. It must be "amazing" and "unexpected."

In December most people on Earth celebrate happenings so rare and astounding that they can be nothing other than miracles. Most of these miracles are events that happened a long time ago, a baby born in a manger, or oil enough for a night that instead burned for eight. There are others too. Miracles have happened before. But there is always the possibility that a miracle will happen today as well. A lion may lie down with a lamb. A hungry child who has never giggled may smile at the kindness of a stranger. The whole world may unexpectedly decide that it is time to sing the same harmonious song.

A great American author named Willa Cather once wrote, "Where there is great love, there will always be miracles." Aha! So that's the key ingredient for miracles. Love! Love in the light of a luminaria. Love in a stable near Bethlehem. Love beneath a tree in Tappen Wood. December is a time of amazing, extraordinary, and often unexpected love.

December is a time for miracles.

Watch for them.

Love,

John

Sounds Like Love
With Mac Huff

One day, one fine day I met a man.
A simple man of unassuming style.
A kind, gentle soul, a heart warm and whole.
His face wore a peaceful, easy smile.
I wondered how this man could feel such joy.
Unsure of the times that lie ahead.
How could this be? What does he see?
With a nod he turned and softly said:

Look around and see the joy that's there, everywhere.
Look and find the light in ev'ry day, ev'ry way.
Listen to the world around you,
Open your heart and let it surround you,
It's never very far. It's right there where you are.
It's the simple song of life I'm singing of.
And it Sounds Like Love.

There's music in the laughter of a healthy child.
There's peace in the fall of the rain.
There's a song in the breeze, hear it dance thru' the trees,
And harmony in a quiet country lane.

In a tree or a river or shooting star.
In the wonder of the sun that warms the land.
A baby's gentle sigh, a mother's lullaby.
In the friendship of a stranger's helping hand.

So, look around and see the joy that's there, everywhere.
Look and find the light in ev'ry day, ev'ry way.
Listen to the world around you,
Open your heart and let it surround you,
It's never very far. It's right there where you are.
It's the simple song of life I'm singing of.
And it Sounds Like Love."

And it looks and it feels
And it Sounds Like Love.
And it moves and it soothes,
And it Sounds Like Love.

Look around and see the joy that's there, everywhere.
Look and find the light in ev'ry day, ev'ry way.
Listen to the world around you,
Open your heart and let it surround you,
It's never very far. It's right there where you are.
It's the simple song of life we're singing of.
And it Sounds Like Love.

TO CLIMB A MOUNTAIN

I flew to Africa to climb Mount Kilimanjaro. At nine thousand feet your muscles start to ache. You're all alone. By twelve thousand feet you're feeling a little nauseous. Inching your way past fourteen thousand five hundred your head is pounding like a convention hangover and by sixteen thousand you're thinking out loud, "For thousands less I could have been in Maui!" At eighteen thousand feet above sea level you can't lift your chin from your chest. You're quite sure that you're going to lose your lousy lunch as several before you obviously have, and at nineteen thousand, with six hundred feet to go, you're crying and panting, wheezing and coughing, praying that somebody with a sick sense of humor will meet you at the top with a luxury Land Rover gracefully complete with sauna and steaming jacuzzi!

It is much like the year of a typical music educator. The monumental journey to the conductor's podium for the final spring concert looms like a hike to one preposterously elusive mountaintop.

Ultimately, you are all alone. Your head is pounding. You're feeling a little nauseous. You can't lift your head from your chest. You think you can't go on. You wonder "Why? For what? For whom? And is it too late to still get to Kapalua Bay?" The weight of the year is on your head and shoulders. You can't breath. You wonder if you might fall. Schedules and budgets, parents, administrators and coaches, like glaciers they move so slow for you who likes to make things happen. Too many students, too many performances, too little time. Your boots are too heavy, too little breath support, no air! You climb to the podium, nineteen inches or nineteen thousand feet, your head is in a vice, but you manage to lift it for a little look around.

It's an awesome place, this mountain, this podium. The earth spreads out in front of you like a glorious tapestry; the hills of Tanzania, the plains of Kenya, billowing clouds below and above, dazzling sun, the gaping craters of collapsed volcanoes, the tenors. You lift your arms. You can still lift your arms. You made it here all by yourself; no cable car, no four-wheel drive, no budget. It's so marvelous up here!

You stand with your arms stretched out. It's all there in front of you. The whole world is in your hands and as you begin to wave them in swooping patterns oft-rehearsed, that world, the mountains, the valleys, the plains, rivers and even the flowers themselves, throw back their splendid heads and SING! They all follow you and they all SING!

You made it.

Beautiful Susie sings because somebody once told her that she bore a striking resemblance to Liza Minelli. (Or was it Lorna Luft?) Cornerback Joey sings because these concerts are the only time that he sees his separated parents together in the same place. From two sides of the auditorium their eyes and ears are for a time, all on him.

Daniel sings because in choir it matters that he comes to school. Math goes on, English goes on, science goes on, but in the baritone section he would be missed.

They are as awesome as the earth, more glorious than the sun; your choir!

And you live there for a time on this, your mountaintop. It's cold and lovely. You soar and float ever higher whispering incredibly profound thoughts, truths, prayers like "my" and "oh" and "oh, oh my!"

Eventually, you drop your hands and sigh and wonder. But your chin is high now. You made it. It's June once more and you start down that formidable slope thinking, "Alas, it wasn't so hard," or maybe it was. Still, "I made it up that mountain again," and "like last season and the season before, I alone made my flowers sing!"

Batoto Yetu (Our Children)

With Roger Emerson

Gather 'round me children,
Gather 'round me little one.
Like the stars around the moon,
Gather round my child.

Do not cry my child,
O do not cry my little one.
I, your mother, am here,
Do not cry my child.

Hush-a-bye my child,
O hush-a-bye my little one.
I , your father, am here,
Hush-a-bye my child.
Hush-a-bye my child.
Hush-a-bye my child.

Batoto Yetu!

From a humble place,
In a humble race they run
To a promised land
With an outstretched hand they come.
Having dreams, they always want to know,
Hearing "yes" but learning "no" they grow.

Batoto Yetu, everybody!
Batoto Yetu hear my call!
Celebrate! Batoto Yetu!
Celebrate! Come one and all!
These are our children!

Hearing what they know cannot be just
Feeling free but needing me to trust.
Seeing poor and wanting more explained,
Having dreams that often seem in vain.

Batoto Yetu, everybody!
Batoto Yetu hear my call!
Celebrate! Batoto Yetu!
Celebrate! Come one and all!
These are our children!

Day. Night.
Wrong. Right.
Big. Small.
They all are our children.

These are our children.

Teaching in Papua, New Guinea.

Teaching in the Philippines.

"Touch the Future" Festival, Germany.

Teaching in Japan.

"Tap City!"
Tap Dance Class in Japan

Thumbs up!

Brother Kevin and
I teach the Hokey
Pokey to students
in Liberia.

Now ***that's*** what
it's all about!

*Red Square
after
a 14,000-mile
ride on the
Trans-Siberian
Railroad.*

The true joy of singing! Sister Judy and nephews Charlie and Cello.

I love this kid!

Moses Hogan, Emily Crocker, me and Mac Huff.

"Collaborators in Choir"

Fred Waring,
mom and me.

Craig Jessop
(Mormon
Tabernacle Choir),
Weston Noble
(Luther College)
and me.

Kirby Shaw
and
Roger Emerson.

Rehearsing for President Reagan's Inauguration.

Staging for "Stand for Children," Washington, D.C.

Connecting with the Youngstown Connection.

Top of Mount Kilimanjaro.

Dancing in Prague.

My 40th birthday party in Greece.

America Sings! does the Macy's Parade.

America Sings! with Mayor Guliani of New York City shortly after 9/11.

SEASONS

Dream Sonnet

When e'er at night alas, I fall asleep,
And journey to a world that's vast and deep.
Where ev'ry wish I have is sure to keep,
And I can count my dreams as well as sheep.

I see the best of all that we might be
And ponder on each possibility
My thoughts meet yours and keep good company
And all is as a dream-filled symphony.

It's true! My friends, I sometimes think of gold.
Or other treasures I alone might hold.
Still most of all alas, if truth be told
I dream of simple joys as I grow old.

At last I ask of ev'ryone of you,
Please do your part to make my dreams come true.

HOPE

It is an easy task to be hopeful when you spend your life around children. They are the very embodiment of hope. After all, when you are a nine-year-old you feel in your heart that things will be even better when you finally reach double digits. When you are a fifth grader, middle school looks like the greatest show on earth! Eighth graders can hardly wait for high school. Ninth graders want to be anything other than a freshman. Juniors want to be seniors and seniors are fairly bursting to get out and take part in the perceived great freedoms of the exhilarating adult world. If they only knew! To be around beings that are always looking ahead to an even brighter tomorrow can be very contagious. You find yourself thinking, "Yes! There are more wonderful things to come, just around the corner." I think that this is why teachers are generally optimistic, hope-filled people. (At least the ones who resist spending all of their free time in a grumbling faculty lounge and focus on the children they are lucky enough to have as students.)

The beginning of the school year is also a time of great, renewed hope. The floors are shiny, well shinier. The walls are freshly painted. (I know, you did it yourself.) The halls are filled with a sense of newness, anticipation, and hope. The principal is friendly, loves music and has tripled your budget! Okay, well the walls are freshly painted. The children generate most of the hopeful excitement. Some are nervous, even afraid. Some are feeling their oats. After all, they're ten now! In truth, some are just so glad to get back to the structure that may be lacking in their home life that relief is side by side with hope. Ah! It's good to be a part of bringing children relief as well as encouraging their natural tendency to hope.

When they walk into the school in their new tennies, (or maybe not) they look with urgency for the familiar; a steady friend, their old desk now occupied by a (pity them) nine-year-old, their locker, a route to class they remember, a teacher who knows their name already. And who is the one teacher that they had once or twice a week last year and the year before? The one that they can count on to be there once or twice a week again this year and the next with their basket of instruments and their familiar bass clef brooch? That's right! It's the music teacher!

"'S'pose we'll start with the 'Star Spangled Banner,'" they knowingly tell the new kid.

"We always start with the 'Star Spangled Banner.'"

"You'll get used to her pretty fast."

"Oh yeah! She's always that perky!"

"What? You didn't have music at your last school?"

"Bummer."

It's true. From grade to grade, in many instances it is only the specialty teachers that the students carry over (or is it run over), from year to year. The specialist has the unique opportunity to assuage fears and apprehensions with their consistent presence, and yes, typical music teacher perkiness. (Pick your own consistent trait if "perkiness" is not your cup of tea.) For even with their hearts and heads full of hope, youngsters need the familiar to counter their apprehensions and make the beginning of the school year an opportunity for a genuine fresh start. It's yet another intensely rewarding role that music teachers get to play.

It's yet another intensely rewarding role that music teachers get to play.

Teachers too, come back to the beginning of the school year with a renewed sense of hope. Perhaps there were summer workshops that encouraged and inspired, as well as provided fresh approaches to familiar lessons. Maybe the hope stems from a good beach vacation, time with your own family or the simple realization that last year's particularly challenging sixth grade class has finally moved on and took Joey Stendahl with them! More than likely it is the sincere love for the students and peers with whom you will take on the new school year. It is also the recognition of the value that kids bring to the table, not the least of which is reinvigorating hopeful outlooks on life. Annually the new school year is a time to evaluate and reaffirm that being a teacher is a grand way to fill a life.

I was deeply touched by the anonymous poem that was so eloquently delivered at the recent funeral service of the 101-year-old Queen Mum at Westminster Abbey in England. As the reader sought to console and inspire the grieving royal family and a world of friends and admirers he suggested:

You can shed your tears that she is gone or
you can smile because she has lived.
You can close your eyes and hope that she'll come back,
or you can open your eyes and see all that she's left.

At the end of the day, the school year, a career, a life, it is fair to consider how well a life has been lived. It is natural to wonder if a difference has been made, time well spent, potential lived up to.

I believe that every time a teacher goes to school and recognizes the glimmer or glare of hope that burns within each child and realizes that it is their challenge and privilege to keep that flame alive for that year and beyond, giving that child the tools to carry their torch out into the big wide world and make it shine; that teacher has made a contribution to the world that can never be overstated or overvalued. It is a gift that makes the world better every single day!

That is why I love teaching. That is why I love teachers. Perhaps on top of all the other duties and responsibilities you embrace every single day, the most important one of all is that you keep hope alive. Thank you for being music teachers. Thank you for giving hope *a place in your choir!*

If I Had a Sycamore Tree

If only I had a sycamore tree
With branches stretched low to the ground.
Imagine the fanciful things I'd see
Up high with a fresh look around.

I'd see where the ocean meets the shore
I'd gaze over daunting hill.
I'd rule like a king or an emperor.
I wonder if I ever will.

If anyone should come my way
I'd lay a path of light.
I'd show them joy in each new day
And keep them brave at night.

I'd be the first to greet the morning sun
You would know the best of me.
I'd see the good in everyone
If I had a sycamore tree.

GRATITUDE

Without a doubt, my favorite holiday of the year is Thanksgiving. Beside the fact that it was started in America, I like it for a lot of other reasons too. First of all, it's just a great time of year in almost every part of the world. The air is replete with the smells of autumn, void of the oppressive heat of summer and not yet beating us up with winter's bitter cold. At Thanksgiving you don't have to do any shopping, except for groceries, send any cards, or even watch the fireworks. (I'm sorry, but am I the only one who gets a sore neck at those things?) All you have to do is get together with your family and friends, eat until you're uncomfortable and count the many blessings that you have.

Hopefully, you also get up early enough to watch the America Sings kids perform in the Macy's Thanksgiving Day Parade live from New York. Unlike me, you can watch it from the cozy comfort of your home surrounded by your family and friends, while one thousand kids and I battle the elements and New York's finest on the corner of 34th and Broadway! I am not complaining, for indeed it is a time to be thankful.

This year I am particularly thankful for my very good friend Julie West. Julie is a music teacher at Palms Middle School in Los Angeles, California. And I dare say, one of the very best. I am thankful that there are people like Miss West who give teaching a good name and students a fighting chance. With her remarkable dedication to students and music education she makes lives better every single day. I am especially grateful to Julie this year because she shared with me one of her students, Dana Mark, or "D.J." to his many friends. D.J. in turn shared with me the story of his remarkable eleven-year-old life. In his own words, D.J. writes:

> *My life has been very challenging but fun. Starting back to when I could first remember, my Mom split up with my Dad because he was not doing a good job raising us. We moved in with a man that didn't treat my Mom good. A few years later my Mom died. I was only five or six. That was the hardest time of my life, especially when I found out what death was.*

As I was growing up I had my right leg amputated. I had to get needles drilled through my bone. Now I have an inoperable brain tumor. I never have and never will let them stop me from having fun. I moved in with my aunt who does a good job raising me. I have a little cousin to look after now. I made lots of friends and joined a band at my school. I'm learning three instruments; the flute, drums and guitar. I will never forget the bad things that happened in my life and I'll always remember the good.

Folks, I'm not making this up!

One of the best things about being a teacher of any subject is that when you have a classroom full of students with problems and challenges of their own there is often little time in the schedule to dwell too heavily upon the challenges in your own life. In a country that is, with some merit, often crit-

> *Good teachers discover and relish that joyous responsibility of looking after others every day.*

icized for focusing too acutely on the man or woman in the mirror, working with young people helps us move the focus from the "me" to the "them." I'm no psychologist, but to me this diversion has quite a healthy ring to it. Even at eleven years of age, D.J. certainly has discovered the joy it is to "have a little cousin to look after now." Good teachers discover and relish that joyous responsibility of looking after others every day. Of course, this is not to suggest that teachers ought to deny themselves the necessity of taking care of themselves as well. Too often teachers forgo their own well-being because the demands of the profession are such and their dedication so great to the needs of their charges. I am a strong advocate for optional, or perhaps even mandatory, sabbaticals for teachers at all levels to rejuvenate, heal and recharge. Hopefully, all of you have found ways to do that even if your school board isn't offering you nine months in Maui to perfect the hula and play the ukulele!

Isn't it great that after the trials and tribulations of his life, D.J. chose to focus on the success he has found playing in the middle school band? Three instruments is a grand measure of success in the eyes of this young man who has already overcome a broken home life, the death of a parent, an amputated leg and an "opportunity" brain tumor. Three instruments and a teacher like Julie West has made that happen, I can assure you.

This Thanksgiving I give thanks for the wonderful friends and peers I get to work with everyday; Roger, Mac, Moses, Kirby, Alan, Emily, John, Cristi, to name a few. I give thanks for my wonderful family; Mom, Michael, Judy, Kerry, Sherry, Steve, Kevin, Jeff, Joan, Karen and Kent to name a few. (I'm not kidding, there's a million more!) I give thanks that I share the profession of music education with tens of thousands of people like you who I am so proud to call my peers; people who look around the music classroom every day, just like my mother taught us to look around the dinner table, to make sure that all are being cared for. I give thanks for Julie West and the gracious winds that guided her into her role as teacher to generations of D.J.s and more. And I give thanks for D.J., and all the D.J.s of the world who inspire us through their hopefulness. Like D.J., I hope that every one of them is someday able to find their rightful *place in the choir.*

We Remember
With Mac Huff

There was a day when freedom's light seemed very far away.
There was a day that looked like night; we dreamed of yesterday.
But even when the day is dark and rainbows hard to see,
Heroes walk among us and people still live free.
We still live free.

We remember the day we all stood strong.
We remember when we were one in song.
We remember,
Remember.

There was a day when Americans chose to take a stand.
There was a day when the best of friends offered us their hand.
The world can still be beautiful but even when it's gray,
The sun will shine upon us and warm our tears away.
And so we say,

We remember the day we all stood strong.
We remember when we were one in song.
We remember,
Remember.
We remember,
Remember.

GOD BLESS US EVERYONE

It's December nineteenth and the annual holiday pageant is not days, but minutes away. Eleven-year-old Mary Beth Reynolds stands in front of the full-length mirror and tugs at the elastic on her tutu, straightening the straps on her ever-shrinking leotard for the umpteenth time. After six years of ballet lessons at Miss Julie's Dance Studio and Baton Salon, she has never felt so oddly uncomfortable. "What's the matter with this thing?" she says out loud to her own reflection, her confidence waning as fast as her youth. "It fit so perfectly last year when I was just one of the sugar plum fairies. This year I'm front and center and it seems like I'm busting out all over!" Bust or not, Mary Beth Reynolds has *a place in the choir*.

Jimmy Fetzer is the meanest kid in the sixth grade. Everybody knows it. He's so mean he can make a veteran teacher cry and a student teacher change her major. He's so mean his desk has to be placed in the corner beyond the reach of any of the other students or any of the erasers he uses as weapons on unsuspecting substitutes. He's mean. Everybody knows it but his mother. Even she has her suspicions. "But it's Christmas!" you think, "surely, he'll be nice at Christmas!" But you don't know Jimmy Fetzer! He's mean all year 'round. Still, Jimmy Fetzer has *a place in the choir*.

Miss Melody is the music teacher and has been for twenty-seven years. She has a dresser full of treble clef shaped brooches and a full-sized bust of Ludwig Van Beethoven on her desk with yellow post-it notes sticking all over it reminding her of everything from students' names to grocery lists. She's seen it all and heard even more. She's produced twenty-seven versions of Ruth Artman's sure-fire rendition of *The Nutcracker*. She's seen hundreds of uncomfortable Mary Beth Reynolds and dozens of Jimmy Fetzers come and go. Nothing shocks her. She believes in the music.

Miss Melody has laid down the law with the parent volunteers. "You can sew, paint, and wipe noses to your heart's delight, but you have no say whatsoever in the choice of music, the way it is taught, or the casting of the leading roles. I am the boss. You are the workers. I am Santa. You are the elves. I am God…." Well, you get the idea. Miss Melody has *a place in* front of *the choir*.

Althurd Said is the jolly janitor/reliable stage manager extraordinaire. The children love him. Miss Melody depends on him. He never speaks. He never whistles. He's silent and solid as a rock. But after Amelia Sylfest the school secretary, Althurd Said runs the school and everybody knows it. He dresses carefully in red suspenders that the first graders love to snap and he loves to let them. He is ready for anything that might arise. He has changed the light bulbs in the twelve coffee cans the school board consider stage lights. He has carefully sewn shut the moth holes in the patchwork quilt that will serve as the main proscenium curtain, and he has double-waxed the floor of the stage in the "No-Purpose Room" so that it shines like the top of the Chrysler building. Even Althurd Said has *a place in the choir*.

The cast is about to take their places for the opening act. Because of scheduling complications there has never been an actual dress rehearsal. The performance itself will be the first time that the entire cast has actually been available for the show. Even that depends on whether or not moms and dads are able, or think that it's important enough, to get their child to school for the performance or not. Miss Melody is fully aware that an eighty-seven percent turnout of cast members in her town is fairly optimistic for an evening performance, and she has planned accordingly with double casting and weekly reminder notes sent home via the student performers.

She is an eternal optimist. But does she really know Jimmy Fetzer?

"What happened to my waist?" Mary Beth wonders with some alarm. "I used to have a waist!" Her reflection shows a box-like figure straight down from shoulders to waist, with not so little bulges here and there where the elastic is threatening to cut off her circulation. "My big night and this body is not my own! I cannot fail in front of my family and peers. I will not fail in front of mean Jimmy Fetzer." Panic has started to set in. It is supposed to be her big night, the crowning achievement following her years of practice.

"Where's my slingshot?" Jimmy Fetzer asks himself, knowing the opportunity will soon be at hand where he could really make a naughty splash. He is dressed as the dashing Nutcracker himself. It was Miss Melody's idea that maybe if Jimmy was given an important role the goodness that was hidden deep in his heart would somehow rise to the surface on a holiday stage. She is an eternal optimist. But does she really know Jimmy Fetzer?

The first few acts go off without a hitch. The kindergarteners are adorable as the dancing teddy bears. The first and second graders are splendid as the Chinese dolls. The third, fourth and fifth graders sequentially knock 'em dead with cuteness and enthusiasm. It is time for the "Dance of the Sugar Plum Fairies," this year led by the swell and swelling Mary Beth Reynolds and her slightly too tight tutu.

Althurd Said watches misty eyed from the wings as the sugar plum fairies ready themselves for their big number on his shiny, waxed stage. Miss Melody thinks, "Two more songs and I'm out of here for a two week vacation on the islands. I might just make it again."

Mary Beth Reynolds takes a deep breath in the wings. Jimmy Fetzer draws back the band of his slingshot from his spot by the Christmas tree, taking aim at the spot where Mary Beth is scheduled to dance. She's ready. He's ready. Miss Melody is ready. The audience is ready.

Exuberantly, Mary Beth Reynolds makes her much anticipated entrance at a full and bouncing ballerina's gallop. She chausses into her preparation, readying for the glorious grand jete' she has practiced over and over in front of the mirror at Miss Julie's Dance and Baton Salon. On her final plie before she takes flight, the effectiveness of Althurd Said's well-waxed floor finally comes into play with consequences that are nothing short of disastrous. As Mary Beth's parents hold their breath and pray for their rapidly maturing daughter to take majestic flight, Jimmy Fetzer releases the band of his slingshot, sending the marble projectile singing toward the lead sugar plum fairy's tutu. Mary Beth's feet slip completely out from under her and she lands hard with her bottom on the shiny, waxed floor, her tiara toppling awkwardly over her right eye. The marble sphere from Jimmy Fetzer's slingshot misses its mark and nails Miss Melody right between the eyes, knocking her out cold from her place at the piano. The rest of the sugar plum fairies go down like a long row of dominoes, and the entire contingent of kindergarten teddy bears break into tears along with Mary Beth Reynolds and her horrified parents. A stunned silence falls over the crowd, except for a slight moan from Miss Melody as she starts to come to and considers an early retirement. Even Jimmy Fetzer is stunned to silence. The discomfort level in the "No-Purpose Room" is Wagnerian, and the gentle tears of the lead sugar plum fairy trickle down her cheek as she sits at the loneliest place she has ever been in her eleven years on earth.

What would happen? Where now is the glorious magic of the holidays everyone talks about and celebrates in programs and pageants around the world, where all is expected to be merry and gay? Who will rescue the broken heart of a little girl's dream and a music teacher's nightmare? Who? Who? And then, it happened.

From his silent perch near the ropes of the curtain, gentle, silent Althurd Said, the jolly janitor and waxer of stages, walks in silence to the place where Mary Beth Reynolds would have landed had she completed her anticipated leap of beauty. All of the eyes and ears of the audience and performers alike are directed at him, wondering, "What in the world will he do?" And, like a bolt out of the blue, like a prayer from the most beautiful soul, like the cherubic voice of Tiny Tim in Dickens' *A Christmas Carol*, Althurd Said cleared the lump in his throat, took a slow breath, opened his mouth and tenderly sang,

> *Let the stars in the sky*
> *Remind us of man's compassion.*
> *Let us love 'til we die*
> *And God bless us everyone.*

Gently and easily, the hearts of everyone on stage and off were softened like the landing of new fallen snow. Naturally, steady Miss Melody slowly crawled back to her place at the piano and began to play the beautiful melodies of Tchaikovsky's *Nutcracker Suite* in a medley form with glissandos and arpeggios as though she had an entire orchestra at her beck and call. Althurd Said offered his chubby hand to Mary Beth Reynolds and helped her to her feet only to be courteously replaced by yes, believe it or not, mean Jimmy Fetzer in full Nutcracker regalia with practically a halo over his head. For no less than three-and-a-half glorious minutes, there ensued a pas de deux of such grace and beauty that it is still discussed as perhaps the greatest instantaneous transformation since biblical times. And as Jimmy Fetzer hoisted Mary Beth Reynolds over his head in a final glorious lift to the wild ovation of the audience and the heavens alike, there was indeed a moment of genuine peace on earth and goodwill toward men.

I'll Care

With John Higgins

I'll care for you.
I will never leave you wanting.
I'll be there for you
When you need a helping hand.
None of us are all alone,
We need each other in the end.
I'll share with you every cloud and every rainbow.
Know this much is true, no matter what you do,
That I will always care for you.

I'll care for you.
I will never leave you wanting.
I'll be there for you
When you need a helping hand.
We're a part of all we see,
The sky, the water and the land.
I'll share with you every cloud and every rainbow.
Know this much is true, no matter what you do,
That I will always care for you.
Yes, I will always care for you.

STILL HOPING!

It's been a long winter
And what will the birdies do now?
They'll fly to the barn
to keep themselves warm,
And tuck their heads under their wings,
the poor things.

It's true! I walk through the garden and break off a twig to see that the sap is beginning to run-the life of spring. The daffodils and crocus are pushing up with their blossoms even while the last traces of snow are still on the ground. A robin hops along and stops to tug on a worm. A squirrel scurries confidently to where she is sure she has buried the last of her loot, no longer a matter of life or death, just bonus past the danger zone. Children go outside without their jackets like butterflies that have worked their way out of their cocoons. Tennis shoes replace galoshes too early to prevent the halls from becoming slippery with mud. Nobody seems to care. At last, out of the dark cold days of winter, spring has eagerly sprung.

Spring, a time of renewal. A time when new dreams take root like acorns and poppy seeds. When all that has been sublimated since New Year's Day is allowed to germinate. Resolutions are provided a ray of hope like the earth is provided a warmer ray of sunshine. A new beginning starts today.

The first grader prints his name in great big letters on fancy lined paper. A second grader reads a book a day using her finger to follow the words. The fourth grade class performs a musical dressed as flowers and weeds, ladybugs and bunnies. The sixth grade boomwhacks in intricate polyphonic patterns unimaginable in September.

Hope truly springs eternal. It is difficult not to be hopeful when spring is in the air. This is especially true for the teacher and the gardener. (It's hard to distinguish one from the other it seems.) How can one not be hopeful when surrounded by first graders reading as though they always knew how, and better yet, kindergartners no longer standing with quivering lip when moms and dads leave them at the classroom door. It's hard not to be infected with a virus of hope when breathing the air of fifth graders looking so forward to middle school. Take it up a few grades. How can one fail to be hopeful around eighth graders nervously anticipating high school, ninth graders looking forward to finally getting past their miserable hurdle, juniors on the verge of being the kings and queens of the hill, and seniors bravely believing that with graduation, life, their own life, is now at last about to begin. To be a teacher is to be surrounded by hope.

Huckleberry Finn (who better to quote when heading into the adventures of spring?), summed up his great adventures by saying it was a time of, "considerable trouble, considerable joy." Does any teacher nearing the end of the school year not recognize himself or herself in such a year's summation? Perhaps this is especially true for the music teacher. Is the list of troubles too long to consider? The rescheduling that means you now travel to five schools instead of three … a day? The new emphasis that has been put on "reading, writing and arithmetic," relegating artistic and spiritual development to second, third or fourth tier disciplines? The parents who ruined your field trip to the symphony? The rescheduling of the rained-out football game to the same night as your fall concert? The reprimand you received for singing thirty-two percent Christmas music instead of the thirty percent dictated by the new school board's regulations? Are there more?

But there is "considerable joy" too. Consider the progress you made with that rascally third grade. Nobody ever believed you could get that crew to do anything and you got them all singing, swaying, and acting like angels. Well, almost. How about the autistic child that could hardly be in the same room as the other children in October, but participated in the President's Day program in February and made a pretty good Abe Lincoln at that? Remember the tears of joy you shared with the sixth grade teacher after the jointly produced *Musical Adventures of Lewis and Clark*? This is the same teacher you nearly wrestled to the ground a week before over a disagreement about set design and costume responsibilities! Plus it seemed like you were doing all of the work and she felt the same way in return. Remember the time you spent with the child who hung around after school because you were his favorite? You were his favorite teacher, his favorite adult, his favorite anything. Remember the music that was happening at the beginning of the school year? "Considerable trouble." But remember the finale of the spring concert when Joey Stendahl's voice changed in the middle of his

Battle Hymn solo and Mikey Sorenson stepped in with substitute glory hallelujahs that surely made the angels weep. "Considerable joy." Why is it when the list of "joys" is posted it almost always is exclusively about the kids? Ah, spring!

For some unknown reason I have been asked more than once over the course of the last couple of weeks, "Why do you care so much about children and their well-being?" I have to admit that I have never given it a lot of particular thought. However, now that May is here and the promise of new life and renewed hope is sprouting up around us, I think that I may recognize the simple answer in the bounty that reveals itself more and more every lengthening day.

Why do I care so much for the well-being of our children? That's a soft ball. Indeed, how can I not? For they, most of all are hope. They indeed, are spring.

Riding on a Cloud
With Alan Billingsley

Floating on a cloud like a magic carpet ride.
Soft as cotton, high above the trees,
How could any sunny day be as beautiful as these?
Riding on a cloud way above the tender land,
Looking down our world seems very small,
But I can see the splendor of it all.

Rainbows greet me eye to eye, birds give way in the sky.
Mountains, valleys, fields and streams, all seem incredibly shy,
When I'm breezing o'er the world on this velvety covered chair,
Watching all above, below from way up in the air.
This is all I ask for when I pray out loud
Just one day, one magical day,
Let me take a perfectly, utterly, wonderfully, awesome
Ride upon a cloud.

FLOWERS THAT SING!

There is a woman I wish I could have met. Her name was Ruthevelyn Emerson. She must have been a remarkable being. I think that because she was Roger Emerson's mother, and Roger is one of my favorite people on the planet. She also bore Richard and Randy, two more good and talented men, friends to me and credits to their mother.

It was Mrs. Emerson who suggested that everyone needs three things in order to thrive: something to do, something to love, and something to hope for (paraphrased from the words of Joseph Addison, 1672-1719). What a simply marvelous trio to contemplate. I have considered it many times over the decades since Roger first related it to me. It seems to me a good barometer with which to evaluate your life and your place in the universe.

In my own life I seem to be surrounded by two kinds of people, music teachers of course, and gardeners, of all things. Considering Mother Emerson's "Three Guidelines for a Meaningful Life," it all makes a lot of sense when I think of gardeners and the fact that they seem to live long and fulfilling lives.

Gardeners always have something "to do." There are seeds to plant, bulbs to dig up, watering and pruning to be done, mulch to mulch and weeds, weeds, weeds to yank.

Gardeners also have something "to love." In fact, they have lots to love. I have watched as they tenderly nurture their plants, pinching off dead heads, loosening the soil around impacted roots, even talking or singing to their charges like a mother sings to her delicate child.

"Something to hope for?" Hardly anyone I know lives with more joyous anticipation for what lies ahead than the avid gardener. Will the tender shoots survive a late spring frost? Will the berry bushes produce? Will the blossoms of the jonquils really be followed by the daffodils, the tulips, then the lilies, poppies, and rhododendrons like they have for years and years and even generations gone by? Who could quit living with gusto when the roses start to bud and green tomatoes fill the vines? Who would not be filled with hope when life is literally pushing up around you?

It is not a difficult leap to see the parallels between the expectant gardener and the hopeful teacher.

"Something to do." The life of a teacher is run by a never ending "to do" list. Lesson plans to write and submit before or after the lesson has already been taught, grades and attendance reports to calculate and disperse, meetings, conventions and conferences to attend, committees to avoid, I mean, serve on. And we haven't even started talking about dealing with the individual and group needs of each and every student. Teachers have plenty to do. No worries there.

"Something to love." That a teacher loves their chosen discipline would seem to be quite obvious. Whether they teach language, literature, history, mathematics, social studies, art, music or any other subject they most likely chose it and pursued it because of their own aptitude and yes, love for the subject. But more importantly, the educator has an entire class of students to love. The big, the little, the loud, the soft, the quick, the slow, the naughty and the nice, there is always so much to love in the life of a teacher. Blissfully, it is also amazing to recognize how much love is coming back at you from the eager hearts of those we teach. Something to love? What's not to love?

"Something to hope for." Like the gardener, not only is there so much to hope for in the life of the teacher (the success of a student, the success of a lesson, the progress of a class, tenure), teachers are literally surrounded by hope every day of their teaching lives. A sixth grader can't wait for junior high school. An athlete or a musician just knows that in the next game or concert they will get their chance to shine. A freshman is full of hope that next year things will be better when he is not on the bottom of the hierarchical ladder. A senior can't wait to graduate and join the ranks of carefree adulthood. (If they only knew!) Perhaps hope is most obvious in the youngest ones. How do they manage to get up every day with such high hopes, such beautiful, innocent, and high hopes? It is hard not to be hopeful yourself when you are surrounded by that optimism every day of your life. Something to hope for? Such is the life of a teacher.

Yes, gardeners and teachers have so very much in common. Each will plant their seeds, nurture and cultivate their young sprouts with love and determination filled with the hope that when all is said and done they will grow into beautiful living things. And for those that "do, love, and hope" their garden in the form of a music room, there is a pretty good chance that they just might grow flowers that sing!

How Does Your Garden Grow?
With John Higgins

Will you give ev'ry seed
All the love that it needs
To become the best that it can be?

Will you care that each one
Has its day in the sun,
And can grow in a world of harmony?

Tell me how will you do, if it's all up to you?
How will you let them know?
Tell me how will you care?
Will you love, will you share?
How does your garden grow?
Tell me, How does your garden grow?

We're growing up like the seeds in a garden,
Growing up to be strong.
Growing up like seeds in a garden.
Won't you take me along? Come along!

Will you give ev'ry seed
All the love that it needs
To become the best that it can be?

Will you care that each one
Has its day in the sun,
And can grow in a world of harmony?

Tell me how will you do, if it's all up to you?
How will you let them know?
Tell me how will you care?
Will you love, will you share?
How does your garden grow?
Tell me, How does your garden grow?

FOR THE LOVE
OF THE GAME

Whoever wants to know the heart and mind of
America had better learn baseball...
—Jacques Barzun

My father loved baseball perhaps even more than he loved singing. From the early days of spring training, through the steamy nights of Wisconsin summers, and until the final out of the October playoffs, Dad would lie in bed or lounge in his worn out La-z-Boy listening to the exploits of the heroic Milwaukee Braves and later, the generally pathetic Milwaukee Brewers. Even when the games began to be aired on television, my dad always preferred the radio broadcast and the colorful dialogue of the commentators trying to keep the fans in the game beyond the seventh inning stretch.

Dad played city team baseball when I was a kid. I can see him now in his magnificent uniform, glove on one hand, other arm draped around my mother, his best friend Bernie, or my Uncle Eldie.

My brothers and I all became baseball fanatics as we were growing up; Kerry at shortstop, Steve at catcher, Kent at second base, Bo at first, Kevin enjoying the peace and quiet of right field and me, an awesome presence at third base. I always played third base from Little League right on to the Pony squad. I like to think it was because of my incredibly powerful right arm that could get a grounder to first base with time to spare, or my intimidating ability to charge a baseline bunt that made batters weak-kneed and pitchers sneer with confidence. In truth, I think it was because I had an uncanny knack for infield chatter. "Hey batter, batter! Swing batter, batter! Your mother wears ..." Well, you know the rest.

I discovered later on in life that my baseball-loving Dad made up words. Like "blookus." That's what you call the joker in a deck of cards. Surely you knew that! Or "hughey." That's when you hit your tee shot in golf so pathetically short that you have to drop your shorts to your ankles and run up and hit it again before anyone else takes a turn. My brother Kent is the only person I ever saw actually do it, but we talked about it a lot. My Dad called it a "hughey." I don't know why.

So to my brothers and sisters and me, a "pud" is a baseball catcher's mitt. I thought everybody called it that until I went to see my niece Claire in a high school girls softball game. In the game that I witnessed, Claire was the pitcher. She's really good at it. Naturally, when the time seemed appropriate, from my seat in the bleachers I stood up, cupped my hands around my mouth and let out a hearty "Come On! Claire Baby! Hum fire! Chuck to the pud! Chuck to the pud!"

My sister Sherry (Claire's mother) quickly grabbed my shirt and pulled me back down to the seat beside her. "Shhh!" She said, "They don't know that word. You're not allowed to yell it."

"What? What word?" I ask in genuine mystification.

"Pud! They say it's not a word. And Claire gets very embarrassed if we yell it from the grandstand."

"What? Pud is not a word! Of course it is! It's a catcher's mitt! You know that, Sherry."

"Yes, of course I know it and you know it, but nobody else at this game has ever heard it before. I think Dad and Bernie made it up." Sacrilege.

"Pud! Pud! Sounds like wood! What do they teach in this school for Pete's sake?"

"John, don't embarrass your niece, you're already hard enough to explain to people."

I sat down muttering "Well, I never." Then I looked out to the pitcher's mound where I could see Claire staring straight at me and mouthing the words ever so clearly, "Pud is NOT a word!" Is too.

The pitcher for my little league team was Allie Solberg. That's short for Allen. (No, this was pre-Title Nine. Since I'm digressing, I do seem to recall my sister Karen pinch hitting a time or two when the roster was low due to summer vacations and what not.) Allie Solberg had a powerful left arm and a miserable disposition. I know this because not only did he pitch with that arm, but he also used the fist that was at the end of it to punch me in the stomach about once a week for four years straight. To this day I have no idea why. Perhaps he was simply annoyed by my constant and grating third base chatter.

Brother Bo's back up at first base was a tall, skinny kid named Steven Johnson. He had the crookedest elbow you've ever seen from some childhood accident and questionable doctoring. His brother Alan played as well, and Jimmy and Tab Kindschy, Chris and Dennis Stephanson, Grant, Mark and Dwight Frederickson, Brian and Lee Nelson, and the rest of the gang. They were good people with whom to grow up. Mom kept the books. Dad coached. Everybody knew what a "pud" was.

I wonder if the world was really as innocent then (the 1950s and 60s), as it seems in my memory. Perhaps. I don't remember worrying too much about terrorist plots although Bonnie Christiansan scared the heck out of me, and with good reason. She was a ninth grader when I was about eleven and shoved me head first in a trash can down at the youth center we called the Red Balloon. I probably had it coming. "Hum baby! Hum baby! Chuck fire! Down the pipe, down the pipe!" Yeah, I had it coming.

I do know that there were kids in my little town who had a pretty rough go of it through no fault of their own. Then, as now, there were broken families and prejudices, children who went without and who had to get by through sheer determination. In a way it's sort of encouraging to realize that the world is not really so different now as then. It really isn't going to hell in a hand basket as we are often led to believe. As we did when we were young, most children still wake up every day believing that what will happen to them that day is the most important thing in the world. Maybe it is. No, not maybe, it is. They go to school, see their friends, sing in the choir, harass their teachers, play a little ball. As well they should.

What does all this baseball talk have to do with *a place in the choir*? My father passed away in October right before the World Series of 1999. The Brewers were so far out of it that there was no need to hang around anyway. Midway through his funeral at Holmen Lutheran Church the entire congregation linked elbows, swayed and sang through their tears the most reverent rendition of the classic sing-along "Take Me Out The Ball Game." It's a song every kid ought to know. Anyway, "Let's take it around the horn, boys!"

Barnyard Baseball
With Alan Billingsley

The farmer went out walking and much to his surprise.
He saw a most amazing sight right there before his farmery eyes.
The animals were playing ball. They all knew what to do.
The sheep was shouting "baaaa"- ter up!
The rooster cock-a-doodle doo that means you!

Barnyard baseball! What a funny sight!
Barnyard baseball! It made me laugh all day and night.
Oh barnyard baseball! Oh what a lot of fun!
The dogs "bow wow!" The cats "me-ow!"
The horse said "neigh!" The goat said "yea!"
The pig said "oink!" The chick said "cheep!"
The donkey threw, the cow said "moo!"
And the short stop ducked 'cause she was one! Quack!!!!
Play Ball!

THE FRIENDLY BEASTS

"I," said the donkey all shaggy and brown.

I like to encourage students to try their hand at making a homemade Christmas present each year for somebody that they care about. It's a tradition that my family has been carrying on for decades. We draw names a year ahead, and have that entire time to make one homemade present for another member of the family. It sounds great, doesn't it? Almost Walton-ish, I've been told.

And indeed in many ways it is. All of my brothers and sisters (all ten) have homes filled with these homemade presents collected over the many years of merry festivities.

I carried His mother uphill and down;
I carried her safely to Bethlehem town.

The trouble is that nobody in my family has any talent for arts and crafts, woodworking, or macramé! (Except of course for my sister-in-law Debbie who is practically Martha Stewart before the fall, and my mother who can make quilts from choir camp T-shirts that are truly works of art!) But the rest of us ... sheesh!

"I," said the donkey all shaggy and brown.

Consequently, our homes are filled with homemade tables with legs that fall off, paintings of still life with bananas that looked like bratwurst, pottery that started as a vase but became a soap dish, knit shawls that were suppose to be sweaters, and refinished furniture that looks, well ... like it needs to be refinished!

"I," said the sheep with the curly horn,

And I'm the worst! I swear every year I'm going to get better. I get a plan! I see something and I think, "Surely I can do that. How hard can it be to make a ship in a bottle?" Really hard is the answer, I find out! "What about a necktie? Certainly I can sew a necktie together for my brother-in-law, Mike." No I can't, I discover! One year I decided to make a cork serving tray out of wine bottle corks. I don't remember that year. I'm telling you it goes on and on. My basement still smells like yeast from the year I decided to make my brother the Reverend Kevin, homemade blackberry brandy for communion. (We're Lutheran. It's been done.) How was I to know that a cake of yeast did not mean the whole jar?

> *I gave Him my wool for His blanket warm;*
> *He wore my coat on Christmas morn.*

The stress this causes is indescribable. We divide the whole process into four stages. (I'm not kidding; we talk about this all year long.) Stage one: get the idea. This is the hardest part until you get to stage two. Stage two: gather the materials. Do you have any idea how many wine bottle corks it takes to make a serving tray? Stage three: make it. Yeah, right! I have NO idea how to use a glue gun! Stage four: wrap it and write an accompanying poem that tries to deflect attention from the gift itself.

> *"I," said the sheep with the curly horn.*

Some of it really gets hilarious. Like the year my dad refinished an old rocking chair for one of my sisters with an accompanying poem that was utterly Olympian in its rhyme scheme. Or the year Steve painted an entire canvas black except for a little red triangle on one edge and gave it the title of "Santa's Round the World Trip!" (The red triangle is Santa's cap we think. Like all good artists, Steve is coy about revealing the true deep thoughts that inspire his creations.) However, I don't think it's one bit funny that my mother has her gift completed and tastefully wrapped by late spring! A good nine months before Christmas! That kind of rubbing it in the face of your procrastinating children is really unworthy of a one time Wisconsin Mother of the Year.

> *"I," said the cow all white and red,*

More endearing to me is the sound of brother Jeff, still hammering away in the basement on some sincere, but unidentifiable, woodworking project until well past midnight on the Christmas Eve, 364 days since we last drew names. Better yet are the gifts that when finally unwrapped on Christmas morning, cling to the candy cane wrapping paper like still-tacky varnish. Forget that. Not like still-tacky varnish; truly still-tacky varnish. One year my brother Kent gave my sister Joan a home permanent, and she let him! There are a lot of these tales. There are a lot of us.

I gave Him my manger for His bed;
I gave Him my hay to pillow His head.

Before you think that my family is a Midwest version of the Ozzy Osbourne family, the homemade Christmas present, as intimidating as it sometimes seems, is a tradition we wouldn't give up for all the expensive store-boughts in the world. It has become a part of who we are as much as bowling on New Year's Eve. (Yes, we do that too.) I've heard that even my brother-in-law Mark (who threatened to not marry my sister if he had to participate in that home-made Christmas thing) actually treasures the thick fluorescent hunting socks Kevin knitted for him one year. Rumor has it he has even invested in a high-quality rhyming dictionary to spice up his own holiday odes.

"I," said the cow all white and red.

By now, almost all of us have an heirloom-quality quilt covering our beds from the year we were lucky enough to have our name picked by Mom. Several of us are blessed to have blown glass vases (or soap dishes) puffed out by our nephew Jesse, and the hiking stick that my sister Sherry carved for me will have to be (in the words of Moses or Ben Hur or somebody) "taken from my cold dead hands" before I would give it up. It's a grand tradition that we all love.

"I," said the dove from the rafters high,

In the end, it's easy to understand why. To give of your dollars is easy. To give of yourself, your time and talents however modest, your energy and commitment and love, is much more difficult. After all, the gift that someone buys and presents, however thoughtful, often pales in comparison to the one that is molded or quilted, sanded or shellacked especially for you.

I cooed Him to sleep so He would not cry;
I cooed Him to sleep my mate and I.

The end of the calendar year seems the perfect opportunity to reflect on the contributions we did or did not make to the world we share with others like ourselves. When all is said and done, how do we really identify a year well spent, a contribution worthwhile? Is a year spent teaching a child to recognize a familiar interval, or master the Boomwhacker® an endeavor worthy of an individual like you with so many talents and so much training?

"I," said the dove from the rafters high.

It would be easier to pursue a career that required less of you as a person, less of the self sacrifice that is demanded of you day in and day out as you mold or quilt, sand, whittle, or shellac young people into better human beings through the art you know and love. You have choices. It would be easier not to be a teacher.

You could make more money and give to the causes of your choice. You could find a considerable degree of satisfaction with quick shot volunteer efforts that would assuage your desire to give but not take the total commitment that is demanded from a professional educator like yourself. You could just go shopping. You could.

Thus every beast by some good spell,
In the stable rude was glad to tell.

Like a store-bought Christmas present, that gift you give to humanity in small doses may easily be appreciated in the short run and forgotten 'round the bend. On the other hand, like the effort it takes to sew a precious quilt, the genuine gift you give of yourself when you choose to use your talents as a teacher will not be put in a closet or sold at a garage sale. It will instead be remembered and cherished forever, making the world a more beautiful place; like a homemade Christmas present.

Of the gift he gave Emmanuel,

This year I'm thinking of making some tasteful birch bark place mats.

The gift he gave Emmanuel.

Come to the Stable

With Roger Emerson

On a cold December night
Shines a star so very bright.
And the angels gladly sing
Of the gifts the shepherds bring.

More to be desired are they than gold, even much fine gold.
For the tiny baby, only one day, one day old.

I will come to the stable, I will come!
I will come to the stable, I will come!
Bringing all I have to share, just a humble shepherd's prayer:
Let there be Peace on Earth! Let there be Peace on Earth!

Wise men follow one by one,
As the star shines like the sun.
And the angels gladly sing
Of the gifts the wisemen bring.

"More to be desired are they than gold, even much fine gold.
For the tiny baby, only one day old."

I will come to the stable, I will come!
I will come to the stable, I will come!
Bringing all I have to share, just a humble wisemen's prayer:
Let there be Peace on Earth! Let there be Peace on Earth!

Children follow that same star
As they travel from afar
And the angels gladly sing
Of the gifts the children bring.

More to be desired are they than gold, even much fine gold.
For the tiny baby, only one day old.

I will come to the stable, I will come!
I will come to the stable, I will come!
Bringing all I have to share, just a humble children's prayer:
Let there be Peace on Earth! Let there be Peace on Earth!

THE CHRISTMAS QUILT

She carefully removed the plastic zippered bag from the chest at the foot of her four-poster bed. She undid the string and removed the red-brown tissue paper that protected the cushy bundle as she had each year since her retirement just a few years ago.

She ran her curved fingers over the pink squares all around the edges made from the not so flowing robes of the first grade angels of cloud twenty-nine. The alternating blue and white triangles just inside them were salvaged from the angels of clouds twenty-five and twenty-six respectively, or as others would remember them, Mrs. Quamman's fourth grade home-room. Ah! What a show!

Oh look! This sparkling gold and frightfully artificial lame from the year the sixth grade girls wanted a more sophisticated look for their *One Magic Christmas* extravaganza, she thought aloud. Nobody looked good in them, nobody. But they thought they did and that counts for something, she supposed. Well, well ... she remembered this challenging group as she traced with her fingers the raised letters of what was once the logo-emblazoned costume of *Santa's Frosty Follies*. What a bunch of rascally elves, every one of them. She shook her head and then smiled. They put on a pretty good show though, in spite of themselves.

Aha. *Forever Christmas*, the aptly named program of 1982. Show must have gone on for four hours. Or so it seemed. Thought winter break would never get here that year. The blue corduroy was a nice touch though. Cheap too. Costumed the entire cast for less than forty dollars. Candle fund.

Oh my. Here's a piece of Santa's crimson velour. How many years did we use that suit? How many skinny boys stuffed with pillows and Christmas cookies filled this magical costume? Transformed them really. Even the rascally-est rapscallion behaved differently after donning the garb of jolly Saint Nick. If she held it to her nose she was certain that she could still smell the sticky caramel corn that Marty Berg squirreled away in the elastic waistband. Marty Berg. He's no longer living around here is he? Is he living at all? Didn't really do very well in the rest of school as I recall. Just not cut out for sitting at a desk and buckling down to book learn. Just wasn't his style. Made a good Santa Claus though, a real good and somewhat sticky Santa Claus.

What's this, black at Christmas? Oh yes, chimney sweeps from *Once On a Housetop*. I see red, green, black and white for the Kwanzaa capes; light blue for Hanukah, red and green for La Posadas. I covered all my bases that year. Beautiful.

Who could forget the year Snapper Johnson wore this furry white material as *Melton the Warm Hearted Snowman?* Snapper. What a kid. His real name was Alan, but everybody called him Snapper. A nickname his grandfather gave him. The story goes that they were out fishing one day and snagged a big snapping turtle. Alan's grandfather said, "That turtle is just like you, Alan." Alan was insulted. "Grandpa, a snapping turtle is the stupidest animal I know. Why, you can chop off his head and he'll just keep on living."

Love piles up.
It sings refrain upon refrain.

"Oh, that's not stupid son. It's just that a snapping turtle thinks more with his heart than with his head. Just like you." Alan didn't really get it at the time. But as he got older he understood what his Grandfather was saying and didn't mind being called Snapper at all.

She rubbed the soft material against her cheek and was happy to have known a warm hearted snow-child like Alan "Snapper" Johnson.

Well, would you look at this? Purple silk. Must have been a wise man's robe or a turban from that genie costume. A genie in the Christmas show. Now that was brilliant!

It seemed she thought about the children the most just about the time of year they traditionally presented the holiday program for the parents and community. So many years and so many programs. So much love.

Love piles up. It doesn't get easier or dull. It doesn't smooth out or mellow. It heaps like snow. Year after year it rears up. It sings refrain upon refrain.

Child after child had come into her life and passed through. She loved them all. Some more easily than others, but all nonetheless. She forgot their names, not all of them, but most. She remembered their faces and those of their brothers and sisters. She remembered their voices, their laughs, their tears, and looking down, even their costumes. She heard their lines in her head. "God bless us everyone!" *It's Christmas, Carol*! "Fa la la la la luh la, la, la!" She loved the look of them and sometimes even the funny smell of them. Especially, she loved the lovable sound of them, frequently loud, but often sweet, too. Over the years they mounted up like the treble clef brooches in her dresser drawer, presents from well meaning parents and eager to please students who just knew they were the first to think of it.

There were hundreds of productions, some almost forgettable. *Santa's Holiday Hoedown*, gingham. *A Holiday Moosical*, brown velvet. *December In Our Town*, a green polyester not found in nature, *The Legend of Polar Mountain*, deep blue cotton, *A Holiday to Remember?* Hmm, can't remember. Must be this denim. Thousands of children. Literally, thousands of children. Love piles up.

And this is what it looks like, a patchwork. All the colors of the rainbow. All the textures, personalities and dispositions humanity has to offer. If you hang around long enough they will all pass through your room. On their way to something. Or not. They leave behind a spirit that will always be there, even after you have gone and new music teachers inherit the spirits of those you taught. And they walk out into something bigger than themselves that they have joyfully discovered through your gift of music. And it just piles up.

She brushed her hands over the odd-shaped scraps of memories and considered the children they brought to mind. Years and years full of children gathering like snow, like love. Carefully she settles the quilt around her shoulders, wrapping herself up in the loving remembrance of concerts and programs, musicals and mischief created by all the angels who have moved on but have retained a place in her heart and a special *place in her choir.*

It's Simple
With Roger Emerson

Like a morning sun
Like a gentle rain
Like a light snowfall
It's simple.

Like a baby's cry
Like a mother's sigh
Like a butterfly
It's simple.

Simple as the song of a singing bird
Simple as a loving parent's words
Simple as the flowing mountain stream
Simple as the breeze through a forest trees
It's so simple.

Just a tiny child
In a humble stall
On a silent night
It's simple.

Mother meek and mild
With a hope for all
Like that little child
It's simple.

Simple as a mother's lullaby
Simple as the dove on rafter high
Simple as a donkey or a sheep
Simple as the baby fast asleep
It's so simple.

Simple as the song the angels sing
Simple as the gifts the wise men bring
Simple as the shepherds on that night
Simple as a star that shone so bright
It's so simple!

Just a tiny child
In a humble stall
On a silent night
It's simple.
It's so simple.

LAVENDER SNOW

I've only seen it a couple of times myself. Perhaps that is what makes it seem so magical. Perhaps that's what makes it so entrancing.

The first time was when I was an eleven-year-old paper delivery boy for the Local Daily News, a twenty-four-page stretch of a journal my father ruefully labeled "The Daily Disappointment." It was. But I still delivered it six days a week for the whopping compensation of nearly four dollars and twenty cents every fourteen days. By the time it was collected the money was generally already used up on Snickers bars and cans of frozen Mountain Dew at Jerry and Bernice Mattison's Dairy Bar, our teenage soda fountain near the intersection of Broadway and Main, our two biggest streets. Five days a week the paper had to be delivered right after school. It wasn't bad. I only had twenty-one papers on my route. I'm quite sure that I could still deliver them today if I had to, and I think I could name every customer and each of their idiosyncrasies if push came to shove. There was Mrs. Harry Hanson. We always used her whole name. I never met Mr. Harry Hanson. (Great Fudge. Approach loudly around the holidays so she's ready with the treats.) Cat Woman (I won't name names but this one was really scary, especially every other Tuesday when it was time to collect the lousy eighty cents they charged for "The Daily Disappointment"), Oswald Slette, the Bluskes, Mrs. Johnson, my fourth grade teacher (Nice lady, mean dog), the Urbergs, the Solbergs and just the Berg Bergs. The Thompsons, the Olsens, the Olsens, the Olsens. Well, you get the picture. It was a living, well, sort of. And it kept me off the streets. Well, not really. It actually kept me *on* the streets but there were only a few, and someone always had their eye on you.

Fortunately, in the editorial department at the Local Daily News nothing important ever happened on a Saturday. Consequently, they, and we paper delivery peons, got a day off. But then Sunday rolled around, and no matter what the time of year, Cat Woman needed her paper at the crack of dawn, which in the north where I grew up is not all that early in December, but it seemed like it. I'd haul my sorry self out of bed at four in the morning (it might have been six-thirty but four sounds better) and

I'd bundle up from head to toe in a muffler and hand-me-down parka, mittens on my paws, and Holsem bread bags in my boots for an added layer of protection from the elements. I'd sling my canvas bag diagonally over one shoulder and across my chest, and with hanging head plod on down to the old library to rendezvous with the other delivery boys. There we'd count out our papers and strike out in different directions toward the Olsen's and the Olsen's and the Solberg's and the Berg's houses.

That's where I first saw it so many years ago, December, four o'clock (or maybe six-thirty), when the sun was just starting to color the eastern sky. There, shimmering in the shadows beneath the leafless elms, their black arms stretched up, out, and sometimes toward you.

There, holding up the carpet of diamonds the last of the moonlight makes flicker where your feet will go down the unplowed road. There it lingers where last night it fell. Not blue, not gray nor pink like the sky, and certainly not white, as you would certainly be right to expect. There. It's pure lavender. Lavender snow.

Things are not always as they seem.

There are no footprints in lavender snow. No dirty tire tracks, no trail from sleds, no snowmobile treads. No scars, just pure, immaculate, guileless snow. Like light. Like trust. Fresh. Like the future. Like hope. It covers everything that lies in your path to the point where the path itself might be lost for a time. It illuminates another way, a myriad of other ways. It covers what's behind you and helps you forget. It beckons you to new beginnings, new trails, endless possibilities beautifully recognized in the refreshing splendor of lavender light.

Things are not always as they seem. Lavender snow helps one imagine. Snow is not always white. Life is not always what you planned. In this reality the world of possibility may more easily be revealed. A quilted comforter of healing down blankets the old tracks and scars of days gone by. It's over. Move on. The path ahead is yours for the making. You forge your own destiny, and whichever way you turn, whichever way you go, it can all be beautiful. You decide. Winter brings each year to a close. Like making an angel in a brand new drift, we revel in it and shake it off. We count our blessings; celebrate our lives with traditions, family and friends. And then, we get to start again.

It only lasts a few moments. It is sometimes hard to recognize. But there it is-a new beginning. In the glow of lavender snow it may be more easily revealed, but what it illuminates is always there for those who look for it and have the courage to recognize it.

I saw it once again many years later. I was in Alaska and had the splendid opportunity to put on every piece of clothing in the neighborhood and sit behind a pack of barking dogs as we swooshed through the woods for a four o'clock sled ride. Morning or night I don't remember. In Alaska in December it doesn't really matter. Once the mush is on, the dogs quit barking and all you hear is their breathing and the pat, pat, pat of their feet as they race atop the frozen land. The Northern Lights were swirling, for the sun was below the horizon. After an exhilarating time, surreal and oh so real, we careened around a corner at the crest of a small-ish hill. The musher put on the brake and the dogs came to a panting and reluctant halt, mouths steaming.

It was then that I looked out through the icicles forming in the tiny slit between my hat, my earmuffs and my scarf. There it was! I swear to you I saw it again! Stretching out forever and ever, like light, like hope, like the future beckoning every good man, woman and child to dream a new world; beseeching each to begin a new day and take a fresh step toward love, joy, light, and peace on earth good will toward men. It is there! I have seen it! And there are no tracks in lavender snow!

A Light Will Be There

With Emily Crocker

In a world full of shadows,
Broken promises and dreams.
When it seems the world is hopeless,
A light will be there.

Like a star above the ocean,
Like a candle in the dark,
Like a dream set in motion,
A light will be there.

There's a light shining in the darkness.
There's a light for all to see.
There's a light shining for the hopeless.
There's a light in the night for you and me.

Like a candle in the window
In a place so far from home.
Like a promise of the springtime,
A light will be there.

Bright as winter in the moonlight
On a bed of fallen snow,
Never fading with the daylight,
A light will be there.

Follow the light!
Follow your dream!
The light will always guide you onward.
In darkest night, follow the light.
The light will always lead you home.
It will always lead you home.

HEROES AND SAINTS

JESSE, YOU TAUGHT US TO RUN

When I was a young performer hoofing my way through undergraduate school summers by singing and dancing at Walt Disney World, I had the opportunity to meet some very remarkable people. Some of them were quite famous. Others were not as well known but were equally impressive in their attitudes and accomplishments. However, of all the people I encountered, perhaps the most inspiring historical figure that I ever met face to face was the legendary Jesse Owens. The Jesse Owens; at one time the fastest man on earth, the man who set world records in the broad jump and the 200-meter race, the man who tied the world record in the 100-meter race and won a fourth gold medal in the 1936 Olympics as part of the 400-meter relay!

He was waiting in the wings, waiting to receive an award for his many accomplishments in life, while we hyperactive singer-dancer types "did our thing" for the audience. And do you know what Jesse Owens said to me as I came huffing and puffing from the stage after performing what I considered (prior to meeting him) a pretty athletic rendition of "Zip A Dee Doo Dah?" He smiled, looked at me and the rest of the awestruck cast and said, "Gee, I wish I could do that." He listened to us sing, watched us dance, and wished that he could do that! Jesse Owens! Imagine that.

Through example, Jesse Owens taught the world a lot about striving for excellence, setting high standards, and achieving goals beyond what many of us can scarcely imagine. In those 1936 Olympic games, and under the condescending gaze of Adolf Hitler, Jesse Owens showed the world that there is no logic to bigotry and no boundaries for the dreams of humankind as he won races both as an individual and as part of his team. Despite the intimidating forces that were trying to prove otherwise, Jesse Owens showed that he had *a place in the choir* of humanity.

Like the Olympic events, part of the value of being involved in a music group is that there is very often a role for the individual as well as a role for the ensemble. As individuals, we sing or play an instrument, striving to make something beautiful, moving, passionate, or just plain fun. When we join with other musicians it is unlike any other gathering of humans. We make something meaningful happen that often changes our very cosmos in unimaginable ways. It may very well be the only kind of human gathering that does so quite as effectively.

When you teach music, you offer the tools and inspiration to your students that allow them to approach that power and tap into its limitless possibilities. Like Jesse Owens, you encourage setting high standards, and provide the tools for achieving goals beyond what most humans consider possible in their everyday lives. Like Jesse Owens, you infuse your students with the ability to dream. And with music's power to touch our very souls, you provide a vehicle with which to pursue those dreams.

> *When we join with other musicians it is unlike any other gathering of humans.*

There is a wonderful subplot that occurred during the 1936 Olympics that teaches yet another invaluable lesson. During the broad jump event Jesse Owens scratched his first three attempts, meaning that he stepped over the line and had all three jumps disqualified. With only one attempt remaining, his chances for victory were slim even though he seemed clearly the best in the field. Prior to his last jump, a German athlete named Luz Long gave Jesse a hint. He wisely suggested that Jesse make his own mark just behind the official line so that he would not overstep. Jesse followed his advice and won the gold medal with that last jump. Luz Long won the silver, and Hitler was furious. Later Jesse Owens commented, "You can melt down all of the medals and cups I have and they wouldn't be plating on the twenty-four carat friendship I felt for Luz Long at that moment."

Music too, teaches us all the value of helping others to do their very best. Musicians' artistic achievements are a benefit to all with whom they come in contact. A person who helps another to achieve any level of artistic expression opens a new world of possibility for that artist. We all benefit from that kind of sharing.

There are people to admire in this world – people like Jesse Owens – who teach us to run, to dream, to fly. And people like you – music teachers- who open the hearts and minds of your young charges to the marvelous possibilities of the world around them. You help them to run, dream, soar, and sing. Most importantly, you make sure they know that they have *a place in the choir*.

Jesse

With Roger Emerson

There was a time when races could never be won.
There was a time when races weren't for everyone.
But in this time, Jesse you taught us to run.

There was a day when all were not part of the team.
There was a day when people were running upstream.
But on this day, Jesse you taught us to dream.

And now we run in a race that is free.
And everyone makes their own destiny.
And we can dream of our day in the sun.
Jesse you taught us to run. Jesse you taught us to run.

There was a night when all couldn't shoot for a star.
There was a night when we couldn't be who we are.
But on that night, Jesse you took us so far.

And now we run in a race that is free.
And everyone makes their own destiny.
And we can dream of our day in the sun.
Jesse you taught us to run. Jesse you taught us to run.

LET THERE BE LIGHT

Who would you choose to represent heroic American women during the celebration of National Women's History Month? There truly have been some remarkable ones – Eleanor Roosevelt, Harriet Tubman, Golda Meir, Sojourner Truth and many, many more.

I cannot think of anybody, woman or man, in American history that I find more astounding than Helen Keller, winner of Brazil's Order of the Southern Cross, Japan's Sacred Treasure, the Philippines' Golden Heart, Lebanon's Gold Medal of Merit, and the United States of America's Presidential Medal of Freedom. Oh yes, and she was blind and deaf. I cannot, in my wildest imagination, fathom being suddenly shut off from the world at the age of nineteen months by the loss of both my sight and my hearing. I cannot comprehend a life of not being able to gaze upon beautiful works of art, on nature in all its glory, a child's face, or even a Brett Favre touchdown pass on a wide screen television set. Moreover, as a lover of music, a life without sound is to me, unthinkable.

And yet, Helen Keller not only overcame her handicaps but soared through a life full of personal and professional fulfillment, inspiring all with whom she came into contact to do better by themselves and their world. She became the first blind person in history to graduate from college. She championed women's rights, fought for the cause of workers and equality for minorities, and became a world crusader for the underprivileged and oppressed. At her memorial service in 1968, Senator Lister Hill of her home state of Alabama said about Helen Keller, "She will live on, one of the few, the immortal names not born to die. Her spirit will endure as long as man can read and stories can be told of the woman who showed the world there are no boundaries to courage and faith." Helen Keller didn't just have *a place in the choir* – she led it.

But how? How did she do it? Helen Keller described the most important day in her life as the day she met Anne Sullivan – the Miracle Worker – her teacher. Life changed for Helen from that day on.

I would wager that every one of us has at least one, if not many teachers in our past that have had profound influence on our own personal and professional development. I have had many. Alice Thomte, my elementary school music teacher who taught me my first dance, the Alley Cat, and with whom I still keep in contact. (I wonder if she knows what a Pandora's box she released?) Jerry Davis, who put me on a stage and said, "make up a dance," Ron McDonaugh, my science teacher and football coach (Yes, I played football and I learned a lot about humility in doing so!), Shirley Radke, Linda Rosso, Everett Berg, and perhaps especially Jan Swenson, my supervisor as I completed my student teaching. The lessons they passed on to me mostly through their own remarkable examples are some of the strongest fabrics that make up the personal tapestry that is me.

If you are reading this, you too are probably a teacher. At the end of the day when you have put the green cloth over the spinet and covered up your traveling classroom baskets, I hope that you know that you are appreciated. I hope that you realize the subtle or profound impact that you have on your students every single day. I am *positive* that you are the miracle worker for someone that you may not even be aware of. You may never get the note from one of them that "made good" and wrote to thank you for helping

When you serve as a teacher you walk in the footsteps and breathe the air full of the spirit of the saints.

them get there. You will probably never be remembered in a will by a gazillionaire who thought they might pay you back for all you did for them. (It might be worth being nice to all of them just in case though!) You may never get the key to the city even though you deserve it, or a Christmas bonus or a Presidential Medal of Freedom. But, you are appreciated and you will not be forgotten.

To be a teacher is not an easy role to play. But Helen Keller was living proof that to attain what is noble, although difficult, is worth the effort for the character and strength it affords. Through perserverance we can overcome great obstacles.

I have often thought that if you tried to describe in one word the greatest figures in the history of humankind, Buddha, Mohammed, Abraham, Confucius, Jesus Christ and more, that single word would have to be TEACHER. When you serve as a teacher you walk in the footsteps and breathe the air full of the spirit of the saints. Not bad company.

I guess it is obvious that Helen Keller understood the power of words. Consequently, what she described as the *mightiest fiat* were just four little words, *let there be light*! That is what teachers strive to do everyday of their lives. She believed that by letting *light* into the hearts and minds of students and teachers, our world moves beyond stereotyped instruction and citizenship into a world where people rise up to think and express themselves, as they work toward a world of harmony. It almost makes me speechless.

So, my fellow teachers, I encourage you to consider the ideas of Helen Keller over and over, and believe that the light you reveal to your wards everyday of your life is recognized and appreciated. Write a letter to a teacher that has made a difference in your life. Ask your students to do the same. Then go forward and continue to be a worker of miracles.

I See With My Heart

With Roger Emerson

If you turn away all you see is part.
Do not run, stay with me
I see with my heart.

You see me as half. I see me as whole.
Do not run, stay with me.
I hear with my soul.

You may be challenged; you may be scared.
I've seen the future,
Don't fear now!

Yes, the road is long, from the very start.
Now I know life is full,
I see with my heart.

We may be challenged; we may be scared.
Look to the future,
Don't fear now!

I see with my heart all that life can give us.
Join with me and celebrate.
We see with our hearts.

COURAGE

Measure me not by the heights to which I have climbed,
But by the depths from which I have come.
—George Washington Carver

There are figures in the history of our great nation that continue to inspire. Around 1864 a child was born to a slave couple on the Moses Carver Plantation in Diamond Grove, Missouri. Shortly thereafter the baby's father died; slave raiders kidnapped the baby and his mother. Eventually the baby was returned to the plantation for a childhood of work. He never heard from his mother again. That little child was George Washington Carver.

Despite the many illnesses and frailties he endured as a child, Carver grew to be a remarkable student of life and a formal scholar who made huge contributions to the world. His thirst for knowledge led him to graduate from high school in Kansas, and college in Iowa. Throughout his college life Carver's quiet determination and perseverance motivated him to become active in all facets of campus life. He was a leader in the debate club and in the YMCA. He worked in the dining rooms and as a trainer for the athletic teams. His poetry was published in the student newspaper and his paintings exhibited at the World's Fair in Chicago. His excellence in botany and horticulture provided him with the opportunity to stay on as a graduate student and become the first African American member of Iowa State's faculty. In 1896, another renowned African American, Booker T. Washington, invited Carver to join the faculty of Alabama's famous Tuskegee Institute.

Through his research in agriculture, Carver worked on improving soils, growing crops with low inputs and using species that fixed nitrogen levels by reinvigorating tired, overworked soil. His keen interest in plants became his life's work and he is credited with more than 325 products made from peanuts, more than one hundred products from sweet potatoes, and hundreds more from plants that were native to the southern United States. A film was made of his life, a museum dedicated to him, a national monument built to honor him, two postage stamps commemorate him, and even a fifty-cent piece was minted bearing his image. But what George Washington Carver really loved to do was play the piano! How great is that?

When I consider George Washington Carver, Rosa Parks, Abraham Lincoln and so many other remarkable characters in our nation's history, the word that comes to mind is courage. Webster's Dictionary defines courage as "mental or moral strength to venture, persevere and withstand danger, fear or difficulty." I define courage as the willingness to step in front of a Junior High School All Boys Chorus and teach choreography!

I also believe that one of the greatest demonstrations of courage is the willingness to believe in the basic goodness of the world and the people around you. This may not be the popular or seemingly wisest posture to some. On occasion, you may indeed get burned. Still, I prefer it.

I am one of the most gullible people that ever walked on this round planet, ("Yeah right, round?" he cynically thought). No really, I believed in Santa Claus well into undergraduate school. It seems to me that we live in a time when many people's biggest fear is that they will get caught being conned. (I admit it. I once sent a check to a telemarketer thinking that I had won a free trip to Hawaii only to be sent instead a bag full of pens with my phone number on them! What was that all about?)

Regardless, for the most part I think it's best to give nature, humans, and human nature the benefit of the doubt. As teachers, I think that it's almost always worth the risk to believe, and believe in, a student even when evidence and experience may tempt you to believe otherwise. This is not to say you have to fall for every line in the book. "No really, we both have to go to the restroom at the exact same time!" or "No kidding! My dog really ate ...." You get the picture. I'm talking more about believing in the potential that lies within each and every one of them to contribute positively to the classroom and eventually to the world. I'm talking about the potential for every student to rise to the greatness achieved by people like George Washington Carver.

All good teachers that I know walk into their classrooms sincerely craving success for each and every one of their charges. In some students it is easier to recognize than in others. But all students have potential, both obvious and latent. It is the awesome challenge of a teacher to believe in and nurture that potential, helping each student discover the unique qualities that can help make him or her successful. I think that this kind of approach takes a lot of confidence on the part of the teacher. Adopting his kind of guardianship takes a lot of courage. If the opposite of courageous is cowardly, it strikes me as such when a teacher looks first to when a particular student is going to fail, as though it were inevitable, as opposed to, "How can I help each and everyone of them succeed?"

A child was born to slaves and orphaned at an early age. The same child, sickly and dirt poor, living in a country so full of discrimination that more doors were closed than open, more avenues blocked than inviting; rises to heights of success and accomplishment known by very few citizens throughout our history. Teachers believed in him. He played the piano. With quiet and indomitable courage George Washington Carver found a place in the choir of humanity. When through his own efforts to get nitrogen back into the exhausted soil of the South left the nation with a surplus of peanuts, George made peanut brittle. When because of your success your classroom is overcrowded with students possessing widely varying degrees of commitment and ability, you make a choir. And you let every last one of them sing! When all others saw inevitable failure you saw potential. You didn't worry about being conned or being labeled gullible. You met a child and immediately recognized that the risk was worth it. That's called *courage*.

> *While writing this chapter about George Washington Carver and courage, unspeakable events took place in our country that made us all wonder if there will be enough courage and honor in us to carry on. I believe there is.*

I do not believe that you can solve every problem in the world with a song. Oh, that it were so. There are events that happen around us that make it hard to believe that the world is a beautiful place. People do unto others in ways that are unimaginable until you witness their cruel reality in the boroughs of your very own communities. When you do it is difficult to imagine what might soothe the pain, renew the spirit and make the world seem beautiful once again.

One of those events happened on September 11, 2001. These were such horrific occurrences that the hearts of our country and the hearts of our friends from all over the world were aching and breaking. That day the unimaginable became ever so real. The events of that hour created such anger, fear, bewilderment and despair, none of which can easily be assuaged with a song or even a symphony. But it also brought to the surface of our land indescribable and countless acts of true courage.

Tomorrow, inspired by these astounding examples of the human spirit, I will remember to live every day to its absolute fullness. I will do the things I've put off for too many tomorrows. I will take time to walk in the park and marvel at every tree and flower. I will make an opportunity to go to the desert and wonder at its stark beauty. I will gaze at the Grand Canyon, listen to the surf of the majestic ocean, look anew at the glorious nature of the hills of New Hampshire and West Virginia, the farmlands of Wisconsin, the mountains of the West, the plains of Texas. I'll hold closely my newest little nephew, Jakob Mark, born on September 10, 2001. And yes, I will sing songs and listen to music. Randall Thompson's *Alleluia*, Ralph Vaughn William's *Fantasia on a Theme* by Thomas Tallis, the hymns and carols, folk songs, and chorales that possess the ability to fill our hearts and renew our spirits. It will all take time. Healing does take time. But in man and music we can find courage. And by next summer when I see so many of my friends around the country at a workshop or such, we will laugh and dance, hug, smile and certainly sing. Yes, sing. And by then, we might all believe in beauty again.

This Is My Homeland
With Mac Huff

Dedicated to the memory of each victim of our September 11, 2001 national tragedy.

"My Country 'tis of thee, sweet land of liberty, of thee I sing!"

How brightly beams the dream in thee, O noble land of mine.
A home that yearns for liberty where freedom's light can shine.
Let ev'ry creature rise and sing, within your heart, let hope take wing,
From ev'ry patriot let it ring, our love of liberty.

America, This Is My Homeland.
I lift my heart and soul to you,
And to this pledge I will be true.
America, This Is My Homeland,
With hope and liberty we sing,
From ev'ry voice let freedom ring.
This is my home.

How brightly beams the dream in thee, O noble land of mine.
Lead forth to build a world that's free for all of humankind.
Thy heroes sound the trumpet call, your boundless courage standing tall,
Protect our homeland, one and all. The noble dream lives on.

America, This Is My Homeland.
I lift my heart and soul to you,
And to this pledge I will be true.
America, This Is My Homeland,
With hope and liberty we sing,
From ev'ry voice let freedom ring.
This is my home.

"My Country 'tis of thee, sweet land of liberty, of thee I sing!"

RESPONSIBILITY

When I was growing up in a family of ten children (in less than ten years for those of you who are gasping), it was a rare weeknight when all of us would be home for dinner together. During the years when we were all from third grade to twelfth grade someone was always at play practice, football rehearsal (I do that on purpose to frustrate my brothers the coaches), church choir, or some other activity that overlapped the dinner hour. So, before any of us could eat, my mother would make a plate of food for whoever was missing and place it in the oven or refrigerator for them to consume when they finally returned home. It was expected that the rest of us would look around the table somewhere between "I fold my hands and bow my head ... and Amen," to make sure that all were accounted for and dinner was appropriated. We were taught that taking care of each other was not solely the responsibility of Mommy and Daddy. Each of us was expected to assume the responsibility of looking out for one another. I often wonder that if everyone in the world would take the responsibility to simply look around the dinner table of humanity and make sure that all were taken care of before they helped themselves, we wouldn't have a happier and healthier planet for all.

Margaret Knight (1838-1914) was a remarkable woman who "looked around the table" her entire life and came up with ideas for making the world better for those around her. One of the places that she looked was in the textile mills that employed many of the adults in her home state of Maine. In those days, factory work could be quite a dangerous job, especially for those who operated the complicated machines with powerful moving gears and parts. It seemed to Margaret that far too many of her neighbors were being injured on the job. Taking on the responsibility for their well-being, this remarkable girl came up with a stop-motion device that could be used to quickly shut down machinery in case of an accident. Her invention resulted in saving many lives and limbs. I call her a "girl" not at all out of disrespect but because of the fact that when "Mattie" Knight took on this responsibility of helping her friends, she was only twelve years old!

Where do young people like Margaret Knight learn about values like responsibility? An even broader question might be where do children learn any of the values that we as a society deem important? Where do children learn that when they see things in the world that do not seem right to them, their response ought not to be, "That's not my job!" but rather, "It's up to me!"

In Utopia, I imagine that the values that we hold dear and essential would be consistently taught within the family unit. Parents, grandparents and extended relatives would take it as their familial responsibility to teach through discussion and demonstration those same universal principles we all claim to buy into. But we don't live in Utopia. In reality, teachers must see it as their responsibility to at least reinforce, if not single-handedly introduce a system of values to each of their students. If not, we risk generations of young people devoid of the best of what makes us human; honesty, courage, compassion, respect and yes, responsibility.

Looking around a classroom or at the faces that make up a choir is not unlike looking around the table at dinnertime.

Oh, I can hear the voices of dissent already! The first is that of the belligerent eighth grader, feeling their oats and challenging any reference to values with the declaration that "I don't have to listen to your values! I've made up my own!" Did they make up their own math, science, history and so on? Of course not. Like those subjects, values must be taught by experienced adults whether they (the students and teacher) like it or not.

The second voice I hear is by a rightfully concerned parent, administrator, or school board member wary of any teacher trying to press their particular personal value system, religion or lack thereof, upon impressionable students. And they have a very valid point. As public school teachers it is not our job to teach the specifics of our own value system in the form of proselytizing or campaigning for our specific, personal, leanings. But we absolutely must take on the mission of introducing and constantly reinforcing the broad universal values we as a civilization have found to be common ground; honesty, courage, compassion, respect and yes again, responsibility.

Gratefully, there is a third voice I hear as well. To coin a phrase, I hear America singing! I hear songs extolling the virtues of a higher system of values. I hear songs about compassion like "I'll Care," and "God Bless Us Every One." I hear songs about courage like "I'm a Lion," " Climb Every Mountain," and "For the Glory." I hear songs about respect like "Check It Out!" and "Celebrate You and Me!" I hear songs about honesty like "Honesty Is The Best Policy!" and "Honesty." And I hear songs about responsibility like "Recycle Rap," "Stand By Me" and of course, "It's Up To Me!" And I hear my favorite mantra, "what you learn through music you don't forget."

As music teachers we have a unique opportunity to teach values and to make them stick. It won't be easy. In a land that puts so much value on an individual's freedom of self-determination and expression, that eighth grader's challenge has become the way of the world. People even older than eighth grade have increasingly embraced the notion that any behavior is acceptable under the umbrella of individual freedom. It manifests itself in discourteousness, littering, lying, cheating, road rage and so many other disappointing ways. But just because it won't be easy doesn't mean we can afford to ignore it. As adults we have learned that often the most difficult tasks are ultimately the most rewarding. Isn't it a thrilling moment in a teacher's life when, after pounding your moral head against the wall to teach seemingly disinterested young people a sense of values, you finally see one of them actually consider and then act with a sense of sincere honesty, respect, courage, compassion or, yes again, responsibility?

Looking around a classroom or at the faces that make up a choir is not unlike looking around the table at dinnertime. It is awesome to consider that the challenge of making sure that each of them is regularly fed the lessons of human values is yours. I encourage you to let none go hungry on your watch. It is our honor and our responsibility to teach just so.

Touch the Future
With Mac Huff

Dedicated to the thousands of volunteers of Canada Sings!

So many stars, and just one night.
So many faces, a beautiful sight.
So many hearts beating like one.
One single planet beneath the same sun,
Reach out!

Brothers and sisters, and friends who care.
Voices to raise and hope to share.
Thousands of dreams sing with one voice;
Standing together, making a choice,
To reach out.

Reach for the future and let your voices ring.
Reach out to each other and sing.
Lift your voice and sing.

We can make a brighter day.
We can make a better way,
When we reach out, we touch the future!

We can turn the world around.
We can find a common ground
When we reach out, we touch the future.

Nothing stands between us. Can't keep us apart.
When we reach out for each other
And the reach is from the heart.

We can make a brighter day.
We can make a better way,
When we reach out, the future is ours!

Tomorrow's close, the time is near.
The future's bright, the dream is clear.
All for one, we'll take a stand.
The time is now come take my hand
Reach out!

Look around now we see one world, one family.
Friend to friend, come one and all.
Change the world and answer the call,
Reach out.

Nothing can stop us. Look what we've begun.
Standing together as one!
All it takes is one!

We can touch the future!
We can touch the future!
Reach out! The future is ours!

HONESTY

There is no terror, Cassius, in your threats:
for I am armed so strong in honesty;
That they pass by me as the idle wind,
Which I respect not.
Act IV scene 3, William Shakespeare's *Julius Caesar*

Almost every day that I'm not traveling I take a break and go for a run through Griffith Park near my home in Los Angeles. It's a refreshingly beautiful refuge in the middle of this megalopolis I now call home. From my house you can run up a wide dirt path to the Griffith Park Observatory, the copper domed landmark that was featured in that James Dean movie, *Rebel Without a Cause*. Once you catch your breath (or have the big one under James Dean's bronze bust) and look through the haze at downtown Los Angeles or west to the Hollywood sign, you can jog down a long winding road back to my house. Along the way you might see a deer, a rabbit, a coyote, or a mugger, depending on the time of day you make the trip. Actually, I have never met any but the most friendly people along the way and on occasion I stop to have a chat with someone else who is catching their breath and stretching their muscles.

One sunny day while running my route, I met Galena. She rocked my world. She was stopped on one of the hairpin turns on the path leading up the Observatory hill. She had her arms stretched out to her sides and was leaning forward from the waist so that she looked like a seagull trying to catch an ocean breeze. My guess is that Galena is pushing seventy years of age. She carries perhaps a bit more weight than most doctors would recommend and packs it into a little less spandex than most manufacturers might recommend. She has chosen the brightest color available for her hair and clearly loves bright red lipstick to match her naturally rosy cheeks and disposition. Galena started talking to me as I trudged up the hill toward her at my uphill jogging pace, which is hardly distinguishable from a walk. She was the most open and honest person I have come across in years.

"I call this my cardio move!" she exclaimed in quite a thick Russian accent. I looked around to see who she was talking to and realized that it must be me, or the bushes.

"It looks like a good one." I responded.

"A couple of minutes of this and I'm ready to go again."

"Okay" I said, slowing to a stop, eager to have any excuse to quit running uphill.

"Isn't this the most beautiful day?"

"Yes. The most beautiful."

"I plan to live a long, long time."

"Me too."

"All you have is your God, your country and your family." This is a woman who leaves very little time for small talk.

"That's it! God! Country! Family!" she reiterated. I wasn't about to argue with her. Nor would I want to.

"Where are you from?" I asked, enjoying her accent.

"I came from Russia in 1961 with my husband. The best man in Russia and now the best man in America. He loves me with all of his heart. The other day I got all dressed up and walked out onto the porch as he brought our old Chevrolet around to the front. As I came down the steps to the car, my husband, he starts to cry. My Galena, he says to me like we are going on our very first date, you are so beautiful. You look like a Russian princess! You should be riding in a limousine not in this old Chevrolet of mine. Imagine me, a Russian princess."

"He must be a wonderful husband."

"Married for forty-four years and he thinks I look like a Russian princess. God! Country! Family! That's all you have."

Galena and I walked slowly up the hill together. I had no desire to run ahead. No wish for the conversation to end. When we got near the top she was breathing with some heaviness and perspiring enough to need a rest. I joined her for a few minutes of "cardio" and then stuck out my hand.

"I'm John!"

"Galena!" she replied, and held my hand for a lovely moment; the genuine gleam in her eyes and the radiant smile on her face making a bright day brilliant.

"You run ahead now. I'll rest here a while." The princess was dismissing me to be alone in her splendid happiness. "Isn't it a wonderful day?" she asked. "Isn't it a wonderful world?"

"Yes," I replied and turned to run down the other side. Truly genuine souls such as yours make it so, I thought, as I ran with my spirits ten feet off the ground.

To meet people so willing to share their happiness and honest feelings is a rare and marvelous treasure. In a sometimes cynical world a voice such as that of my own neighborhood "Russian princess" is priceless indeed. Now, every day when I run I look for Galena. I have not seen her again, but I truly hope I will.

William Shakespeare wrote a lot about honesty through his many characters. The line from Julius Caesar at the beginning of this chapter is a particularly good one I think. Another one of my favorites comes in Act III of *All's Well That Ends Well*, when Mariana states, "No legacy is so rich as honesty." How utterly correct this is, especially for a teacher in search of a legacy. Of course, good ol' Bill also quilled "Every man has his fault, and honesty is his," in his play *Timon of Athens*. That may be one of the reasons you don't see that play performed often.

How do we tackle the character issue of honesty? I'm not going to lie to you. I think it's a tough one. However, whether it is historically accurate or not, the lesson to be learned from the tale of George Washington cutting down the cherry tree is that, not being able to tell a lie is admirable! One hundred percent honesty ought to be the goal for all of us as humans, and certainly the lesson we should be teaching children. God, country, and family are all you've got, and honesty toward any one of them is the least they deserve. Teaching children that honesty still is, and always will be the best policy is not an adage that has somehow gone out of style in some overly permissive society. Teaching them that the quality of a life filled with honesty, even when it hurts, is still very much in fashion in our book. "No legacy is as rich as honesty." No bank account padded, no relationship elongated, no career enhanced will be one hundred percent rewarding unless it is achieved through honest means.

What does this have to do with teaching music? Everything. Through our efforts as music teachers we all hope that we can use our teaching skills to help children become better artists, and ultimately, better citizens of the world. Through our efforts we hope that they will come to recognize that the greatest work of art is not the one that achieves its effect through bells, whistles, red herrings, and shadows. Rather, profound art is the simple or complex product of an artist who seeks and discovers the honest core of the work at hand. Through purely honest artistic efforts we can teach children the virtue of that degree of honesty in the rest of their lives. They will learn that truth is truth and honesty in the arts as well as in life is worth the effort. As teachers it is our job to encourage them to dream their dreams and then pursue them in fervently honest means. In this way we hope that our students find *a place in the* honest *choir* that sings, dreams, and works for a better world.

God! Country! Family! It's all we have. Thank you Galena, for reminding me. Honestly.

The Cry of the Child

With Mac Huff

A Child is born on a blessed morn,
A beautiful baby boy!
A child is born on a golden morn,
A beautiful baby girl!
Could be a pauper, might be a king.
Let them know love and they'll sing!

God hears the cry of the child.
List'ning to their humble prayer,
His song is everywhere.
God knows their hearts one and all.
Keeps them safe, away from harm,
Wrapped in His loving arms,
God hears the cry of the child.

Soft lullabies, closing their eyes
Sweet tales to put them asleep.
Dreams in the air, each little prayer,
A precious soul to keep.
Each one an angel, each one a king.
Let them know joy, and they'll sing.

God hears the cry of the child.
List'ning to their humble prayer,
His song is everywhere.
God knows their hearts one and all.
Keeps them safe, away from harm,
Wrapped in His loving arms,
God hears the cry of the child.

Blessed be the pure of heart,
The meek the mild that do their part.
Blessed be the one who cares,
The one who smiles, the one who dares!

God hears the cry of the child.
Listen to their humble prayer,
His love is everywhere.
God knows their hearts one and all.
Keeps them safe, away from harm,
Wrapped in His loving arms
Come hear the cry of the child!
God hears the cry of the child!
Come hear the cry of the child!

WHO ARE YOU?

Who are you?

It was still dark outside this morning when I saw you through that thin, vertical window at the side of the building; the window that only lets significant light in for a few minutes a year when the sun is at just the right angle in the sky. I saw you in there all by yourself with forty-four tiny violins spread at your feet. You seemed to be trying to tune them, or repair them, or both. All of them, all forty-four of them.

Who are you?

Not ten minutes later, still dark, around six-thirty I think, cars started pulling up to the building. What looked to be dozens of fifth and sixth graders pour out of their parents' SUVs and vans with backpacks as big as themselves. They made a beeline for that room you were in with the pointless window. Just as you swept the violins off the floor, they stormed the place, tossing jackets and scarves, boots and school supplies in random heaps all over the room. They were full of stories of yesterday's exploits. They smelled like Cheerios and hash browns. They surrounded you like Lilliputians. You listened to every one of them. You smiled, joked, patted a head, complimented a sweater, and fussed at a straggler. Suddenly you clapped a rhythm and they mimicked it exactly. Well, almost exactly. They became relatively quiet and lined up on the rickety risers on one side of the room. I watched you. You led them in half an hour of singing and dancing, clapping, swaying, skipping and playing. I didn't know that you could do that, but I saw you.

Who are you?

I heard a bell ring. Your fifth and sixth graders scurry around to retrieve their belongings. You took a sip of the coffee that had been cooling on your desk for at least forty-five minutes. Yum. And I swear, I'm not making this up, in came another batch! This time they were littler, kindergarten perhaps, or maybe first grade. You sat right down on the floor with them.

You knew all of their names. Well, once in a while I think you may have called them the name of one of their older siblings, but they always corrected you and didn't seem to mind at all. They adored you. Together you sang songs and you showed them a little something about the value of musical notes. In twenty minutes or so you did about eight activities. You were a model of efficiency. Up they jumped and walked out the door singing a "good-bye" song while what looked like second graders marched in singing a "hello" song. Twenty minutes later the second graders marched out chanting a rap about dynamics while the fourth graders came in rapping a counter rhythm about key signatures. This went on all day! One group came in, another group went out. You were the constant. Like Winston Churchill, you never, never, never gave up.

Who are you?

At lunch I thought I would see that you would get a break, maybe go out with some of your friends and colleagues to a nice restaurant or find a quiet place for a relaxing picnic. No, not you. Your room was filled with students of all ages checking out instruments, showing you their favorite CDs and dance moves. They ate their lunch in your room as you tried to fix your frozen desktop computer. A third grader finally fixed it for you, his fingers only a little sticky with peanut butter. As your thirteen-minute lunch ended I thought I noticed the words "prep. period" on your calendar. Whew! What a relief. But as the lunch crowd dispersed I witnessed that a high school boy you seemed to know sidled into the room with a worried look on his face. You invited him to stay and chat. You talked about his life. He has dreams of staying involved with music for the rest of his life. You know his parents are not thrilled by the idea. He shares his own reservations in choosing music as a career. You counseled him, reassured him, and encouraged him. He left with a huge smile and a spring in his step. Your "prep. period" was over.

Who are you?

I noticed that the last of the classes jived out of your room at the end of the school day. I watched to see you collapse. You didn't. You didn't have time. Dozens of middle schoolers parade in with Broadway Junior scripts in hand. All of them, and I mean all of them, are singing at the top of their lungs "a daaaaaaaaay….aaaaaa………..waaaaaaaaaaaaaay!" You smile, or grimace, it's hard to tell, sit down at the piano and run rehearsal. There is singing, staging, lighting, and choreography. During an extended piece of dialog I'm quite sure I saw you pull out a needle and thread and start sewing on the patches of an orphan's costume!

Rehearsal ends. I watch as you dash out of the building to your car. Then I watch you dash back into the building to retrieve your keys from the lid of the piano, and dash again to the car in which you try not to speed over to the First Presbyterian Church. Adults are waiting for you. On the way you wonder if anyone picked up your own children from their respective after-school events. With guilt you realize they'll have to fend for themselves. Church choir is eventually over and after an extra rehearsal with the soprano who needs your accompaniment for a weekend wedding, you climb back into your car and head back to school.

Who are you?

Back at school you direct a group of eye-rolling sixth graders through a DARE ceremony. They were providing the music. Actually, you were providing the music and they were mumbling at the floor. When all is over, their parents pick them up exactly at the nine o'clock appointed hour. That is, all except for one. I see you there with one young lady whose parents seem to have forgotten the "appointed hour." "It was on the sheet," you think through gritted teeth. Still, I see you. You sit there on the front step of the school with her. She doesn't have much to say. "Yes. I told them nine o'clock. Yes, I know this has happened several times before. Yes, I know you have other things to do." But you sit there. You even end up having a nice little visit. You share your World's Finest Chocolate with her. Her frantic Mom eventually shows up with little concern. You wave, stand up, stretch your tired back. "Goodnight Joe," you call to the nighttime janitor and stroll back to your car with strains of "N.Y.C." stuck in your head. I can almost read your mind as you think to yourself, "Now that was a pretty good day."

Who? Who in the world are you?

Ah! The music teacher! I should have known.

God Put a Song in Me

With Alan Billingsley

God put a song in me,
A song that is easy to sing.
It's never too high and it's never too low.
It stays in my heart ev'ry place that I go.

Oh, God put a song in me,
It's never too loud or too soft.
When we sing together She adds harmony,
'Cause God put a song in me.

God put a song in you
A song that is easy to sing.
It's never too high and it's never too low.
It stays in my heart ev'ry place that I go.

Oh, God put a song in you,
It's never too loud or too soft.
When we sing together, it's easy to do.
'Cause God put a song in you.

OPEN THE FLAPS: LIGHTEN THE LOAD

January 1994, four o'clock; that's in the morning. I had only lived in California for a couple of months when I was awakened by the wrenching and jolting of an earth that seemed determined to reject me like a bad organ transplant and send me packing right back to the Midwest. The house was shaking like a carnival ride with me as it's unwitting passenger. Everything was crashing to the ground around me as I stood in the doorway and screamed, "Mommy! Mommy!" I was a grown man. It was not pretty. I was not brave. I was not pretty. Welcome to California! Happy New Year 1994!

When the earthquake took a breather I did what every pamphlet on the subject tells you not to do. I lit a match. With my candle flickering I slowly made my way through the wreckage to assess the damage to house and home. Every picture was off the wall, the glass smashed, the frames collapsed. Bookshelves were overturned and emptied. Lamps were tossed to the floor and broken into unrecognizable shards of bulb and psychedelic lava. The medicine cabinets in the bathroom were emptied out onto the floor. Flintstone vitamins were everywhere! The kitchen was the worst. Every single item was regurgitated from the refrigerator and smashed onto the floor. Like one of my best undergraduate recipes, syrup ran together with ketchup, which ran together with eggs and cheese and mayonnaise and orange juice and carryout Asian food that was only a few weeks old. There were concoctions mixed together that even I wouldn't eat, and I eat about anything. From the cupboards every single glass, plate, bowl, cup and saucer were thrown onto the floor by some angry ogre of terrestrial madness, smashed into pieces of a million or more. All of my priceless flatware was ruined. It was devastating. Do you have any idea how long it took me to save S&H stamps to get a full set of Rocky and Bullwinkle CorningWare plates? In a few wild moments, all of my treasures were destroyed. It felt great!

Don't get me wrong. It didn't feel great that morning. It didn't feel great as the long process of cleaning up dragged on and on for weeks and weeks. And of course it did not feel great that people were injured, left homeless, and a few even killed by what came to be known as the Northridge

Earthquake, a name I take some exception to in that I'm quite sure that my house was the very epicenter of the whole affair. It had to be. It simply had to be. The so-called Northridge Earthquake gave new meaning to the words "hop 'til you drop" in my home!

In a few wild moments, all of my treasures were destroyed.

What felt great was that once the clean up was complete and the garbage bins hauled to the dump, there was this wonderful sense of a load being lifted. There was the relief of finally getting rid of all the accumulated stuff you had been saying you were going to go through and get rid of someday. Mother Earth in her shockingly efficient way did the painful sorting for you in a few quick minutes. There were times of near weakness on my part. Sometimes over the course of the next few days I might find a piece of something that only had a small chip in it and I would think, "Well maybe I could still use this." Then an aftershock of four or five on the Richter scale would jolt it out of my hands or off a ledge and make the decision final once and for all. It was gone. In the end it really did feel good; lighter.

Artist Georgia O'Keefe used to say that about every seven years or so one ought to open the flaps on your tent and let the wind blow through. Save the wheat, but let the useless chaff fly away with the western wind. Wind, earthquake, spring-cleaning; whatever the method the result can be the same; lighter.

One of my favorite humans on the planet is my friend Helen Freeman from Camp Verde, Arizona. She is a music teacher. (Why is it that almost all of my favorite people are?) She is the mother of ten children, and as a teacher to the community, the surrogate for many, many more. She is indomitable of spirit and full of joy and wonder from head full of hair to toe. She is the kind of person every child and every adult, every teen and every senior citizen ought to spend a lot of time around. I do whenever I get the chance. I always come away awed and renewed.

This year Helen Freeman's house burned to the ground as family and friends stood hopeless to help. Thankfully nobody was hurt, but all of her family's possessions went up in a whirling cloud of smoke.

I saw Helen a few months later at the summer workshop I did in Salt Lake City. She drove many hours to get there to sing, dance, and share her energy with me and the rest of the participants. I asked her how she and her family were faring since the devastating fire. She replied in the way that I should have known she would. "Oh," she said, "in many ways it's a wonderful feeling to be free of the burdens of earthly possessions, most of which you never use, most of which you never need. The only thing I feel really bad about is that I lost all of my John Jacobson videos and music." Ya gotta love that woman!

Granted, earthquakes and fires are perhaps overly dramatic means to clean out your bulging closets. Hiring a choir as a cleaning crew for a day ought to be far less traumatic. But it's a new year. The new year always seems like a good time to "open the flaps" and rid yourself of the extra bulk; the bulk not only in terms of possessions but in regard to the personal and professional weights and burdens that may be slowing you down in life as you make your way through the world. It's a opportune time to rid yourself of debilitating frustrations that may have built up regarding relationships with peers and administrators, lack of facilities and budget, feelings of not being understood or appreciated, unresponsive students and parents, overzealous booster clubs that didn't like your programming for the winter concert, and any other psychological and emotional burdens that seemed to be weighing you down as the prior year came to an end.

As human beings we are allowed the luxury of being able to reinvent ourselves as often as we wish or as we deem necessary. Give yourself permission to do just so this year. Try something new in your classroom or in your personal life. Make a list of two, three, or ten thousand things that you didn't like about how things stood in your personal or professional life at the end of last year and do your best to earnestly divest or modify them. Give those around you a chance to do the same. Open yourself up to their efforts as well as your own. Especially in terms of the students that are entrusted to your care, with this new year try to look at each of their faces in a new light. Hear their voices with fresh new ears. Forget who their older siblings may have been and refrain from holding them accountable for anything from their past. Give them and yourself a break from any past indiscretions, real or imagined. After all, if we were all held accountable for the way we acted in our youth and childhood, most of us would be in deep trouble, or at least in very deep embarrassment. Every kid, you included, deserves the chance to start all over on an even footing with the rest of the world as often as necessary. A new year seems a perfect time to encourage it.

Open the flaps. Let a new and renewing wind blow through and take the chaff along with it. Face the choir and the world lighter. It might feel great! Right, Helen?

A new beginning starts today!

A New Beginning

With Roger Emerson

Dawn!
A new day! A fresh start!
It's morning.

Light!
The first light.
A young world adorning.

Fueled by a heavenly spark; led by one beacon of hope.
Moving away from the dark to the light.
To the light!

A new beginning will start today.
A chance to change and learn and know a better way.
A new beginning will start with me.
We'll find a way each day to change our destiny.
A dream that ev'ryone can share and see the light from anywhere.
A new beginning starts today.

Stars!
A bright star.
A new dream revealing.

Life!
A young life.
A new hope of healing.

No one is ever alone. Nothing is ever the same.
Together we'll start moving on and on and on and on and on.

A new beginning will start today.
A chance to change and learn and know a better way.
A new beginning will start with me.
We'll find a way each day to change our destiny.
A dream that ev'ryone can share and see the light from anywhere.
A new beginning starts today.

Dawn! A new day!
A fresh start!
Good morning!

TOGETHER WE ARE BETTER

My father had about the best final words I have ever heard. It's been a few years now so I can talk about it and even slap my knee at the thought. (I expect that my final words will probably be something like "point your toes" or "keep smiling" so I really appreciate a profound final effort.) My father did it right, and summed up so much in his sensational, final utterance. You see he was a teacher who became a principal, and then a superintendent of schools. His last official act on this planet was to give a speech to a group of elementary school students at the dedication of their new school. He was retired already and not in great health, but he couldn't pass up the chance to teach children, especially if it meant talking about one of his favorite topics, education. He used this particular opportunity to tell these students the history of public education in America. He explained to them in words they could understand, how our forefathers recognized that public education for everyone was the surest way to make our nation great. He was clear, concise and engaging like a good teacher should be. Then he got to the part where he was going to talk to the kids about some of the challenges confronting public education in our country today. He leaned forward on the podium, and gazing directly into the eyes of the children said in a quiet and serious voice, "Now this next part gets a little complicated...." and with that, my father fell backwards into the arms of his Maker, and shot directly to heaven where I expect he finished the sentence in front of a rapt and heavenly group of middle-schoolers, his favorite place to be. "Now this next part gets a little complicated...."

Wow! Dad, you said a mouthful. Someone much smarter than I could do an entire doctoral thesis on that one, perhaps examining theories of existentialism versus fundamentalism or nihilism, or some other "ism." Someone probably already has. But sticking to the topic, let's just see how those words pertain to public education here and now. It is complicated. There are so many theories being discussed today. The pros and cons of charter schools, methods of assessment and their roles in our classroom, teaching to the tests, vouchers; yes or no? Leave No Child Behind (a phrase embraced by smart people on both sides of the wrangling), and on and on. You bet it's complicated!

Not so long ago the mayor of Los Angeles decided to decorate the lamp-posts of the streets with banners. They were rectangular flags with hand-prints of many colors on them and a simple message that stated "Together We Are Better." In Hollywood where the stars work, and in Beverly Hills where they live, in south central neighborhoods filled with new Americans from all over the world, in Little Saigon, Little Italy, Little Armenia, Little Ethiopia, Korea town, Chinatown, Thai town, near the beaches of Venice and Malibu and everywhere in between, "Together We Are Better" was the motto and charge chosen to remind everyone that our community thrives more effectively when we recognize our need for each other, working and living toward the common goal of human harmony.

Perhaps even more poetic is one of my favorite proverbs of all time. It comes from Africa but certainly is universal in its lesson.

"If you want to travel fast, travel alone;
if you want travel far; travel together."

We need each other. We almost always do better when we recognize this fact and embrace it in all of our endeavors.

In the early days of rural America, when a farmer needed a new barn all of the neighbors would get together for a day and have a barn raising. It was obvious that with many hands working together the building could be erected in a fraction of the time it would take if one person attempted this daunting task alone. On first consideration that would seem to contradict the proverb that I just quoted, "If you want to travel fast, travel alone; if you want to travel far; travel together." In this case, the workers obviously accomplished the task at hand much more quickly, precisely because many hands make fast work. But let me suggest for a moment that perhaps the most valuable finished product of a barn raising is not a barn at all. Instead, the real golden harvest of an effort such as this is the community that is built by the combined effort of people coming together, working to do something good. Yes, there is now a useful barn where once there was only a barren plot. But even more importantly, human beings have combined their efforts, each bringing to the table (or in this case the sawhorse) their unique gifts and talents to accomplish something worthwhile. In the end, it is the relationships built through this effort that are the real bounty. Hence, when one is in need, that one will have many with whom they know they can rely, be it to aid in a crisis, offer support, rally a defense, raise a barn, or raise a child.

Aha! To raise a child! Perhaps another African proverb that suggests, "It takes a village to raise a child" has been overused and politicized of late to the point where its profound message has been lost or corrupted. But we know that it is essentially true. When it comes to nurturing the development of children it is the combined efforts of parents, grandparents, aunts and uncles, peers, community leaders and teachers that create the best recipe for success. When all who come in contact with any given child always put the best interests of that child in front of their own contributions to the world, that child has the best chance to go far. Taking to heart the responsibility of raising all the children may be the most important role adults play in society. "It's not the economy stupid, it's the kids." That's a Jacobsonion proverb.

We must keep our eye on the prize that is a well-adjusted, healthy, happy educated child.

What teacher has not been called "Mommy" by a student, much to the embarrassment of both teacher and student? But in truth the roles of parent and teacher are very closely related. There is a lot of overlap, especially in today's world of single parent families, both parents working, children raised by relatives other than their biological mother or father, and so on. Like it or not we all play multiple roles in children's lives. It's easy to get frustrated by any adult member of society that doesn't seem to be pulling their weight or fulfilling their obligation to the children, especially parents. But it's important to remember that it is *never* the child's fault. Never. They are children. We are adults. We are the village and it is our responsibility to make raising *all* children our priority. We must keep our eye on the prize that is a well-adjusted, healthy, happy, educated child. Like raising a barn alone, it can seem overwhelming and yes, complicated.

Nobody is asking us to do it alone. There is a village, in fact a world that is ready to help. The combined efforts of teacher, parent, administrator, aide, professional, laborer, neighbor, and friend must work together to prepare the children in our lives for the road that lies ahead. We do it when we teach them to be honest, courageous, respectful, sensitive, and human. We do it when we make certain that each and every one of them has a place in the choir that sings and lives in harmony. No matter our church, our voting record, our neighborhood, our aspirations, we combine our efforts and work together for the benefit of every single child. Because we know that "together we are better." There's another quote of my father's that I like to remember. He believed it full heartedly. I do too.

There can be no greater yearning in man's heart than the sincere yearning for peace on Earth, good will toward men. Ah! The Quest.

At the River

With Roger Emerson

Composed for The International Celebration Choir on the occasion of the
"Opening Ceremonies of the Bluewater Bridge Second Span: A New Link to Old Friends"
Sarnia, Ontario Canada/Port Huron, Michigan, U.S.A., July 12,1997.

Shall we gather at the river, where bright angel feet have trod,
With its crystal tide forever flowing by the throne of God.
Yes! We'll gather at the river. The beautiful, the beautiful river.
Gather with the saints by the river that flows by the throne of God.

It's time for the world to start again,
Not for a child to wonder when life gets beautiful.
And it's time for a new tide to rush in
And a new day to begin to be beautiful.

So let's meet at the river that flows across our land
And together we'll proudly stand.
On its way to the sea it's a sign to the free,
And we'll greet her hand in hand.

Just for now, as the land is divided
By the tireless colliding of the drops of rain.
And for now, let us all move together,
Like a stream that flows forever, or a midnight train.

Let's meet at the river that flows across our land
And together we'll proudly stand.
On its way to the sea it's a sign to the free,
And we'll greet her hand in hand.

Together we are stronger, together we've begun.
Like a river moving onward, we are one.
We are one! Yes! Yes!

MUSIC MAKES
THE DIFFERENCE

At my funeral I want a choir, a beautiful woman and a boy soprano to sing "Pie Jesu" from Andrew Lloyd Webber's *Requiem*. I'm making certain that I put this in writing for all to see because I'm afraid that everyone will forget to do it and there will not be sufficient weeping and wailing to convince me of the congregation's sincerity and perhaps persuade the Final Judge to go easy on me. I'm hoping that he'll show some leniency and not send me to "Show Choir Hell" where everyone is forced to perform unlimited, alternating box steps and elastic starbursts. Music such as "Pie Jesu" can make that kind of difference.

When I went to the dentist a few weeks ago he told me to bring along my favorite compact disc to play over the headset while he drilled away on my lower molars. I'm usually a white knuckler, but on this occasion, I didn't feel a thing. It's amazing how effective a distraction, a shot of Novocain and Richard Simmon's "Sweating to the Oldies" can be! Music is what made the difference!

I have a handwritten letter in front of me from a high school junior named Tim. He's trying to decide how to spend the rest of his life; what to study, where to direct his energy, how to contribute to this world he's inherited. After much nervous vacillation between one option and another, four beautiful words leap from the page and indicate his heartfelt decision. "What it boils down to Mr. Jacobson, is that I go to school everyday because I want to sing!" Me too Tim, me too!

I am so encouraged by the National Commission on Education's recent drive to prove to our legislators, school administrators, school boards and tax payers that, "Just as there can be no music without learning, no education is complete without music. Music makes the difference." This simple credo is accompanied by letters to support the role of arts in education by such high-powered personalities as the chief executives of MacDonald's, AT&T and Sara Lee! Bravo!

We as music educators understand the importance of music in everybody's life now, in the past and in the future. Warriors have gone to battle to it. Athletes warm up to it. Joggers jog to it. Bikers bike to it. Writers write to it and thinkers think to it. Dentists drill to it. Barbers clip hair to it. Babies get born to it. People get married, ferried and buried to it. It heightens every experience. Children learn the alphabet to it, addition to it, the names of the states and even world history to it. We know that!

Most importantly, music is a healer. It touches where nothing else can reach to nourish weakening spirits and bolster broken hearts. It is not an "extra." Music is THE difference!

Music is not an "extra."
Music is THE difference.

We need not convince each other of music's importance. But we do need to convince others whose support and pocketbooks may not be as easily approached by way of their hearts and souls. To them the justification must be more black and white, less esoteric, more bottom line. So, here are some facts (I made them up) that everyone should know.

In the year 2000, sixty thousand teachers taught music to an average of two hundred students each for approximately twenty-five minutes a day for thirty-six weeks. The bottom line: because of their time-consuming involvement in music, one million, six hundred thousand children were saved from the perils of drugs, boredom, truancy, depression, abuse, etc. for a gazillion hours a day and were put in touch with the positive healing powers of music. This is not a joke, not a joking matter, but a fact.

In 2000, millions of collections, tapes, cassettes and videos were produced, marketed, and sold in North America at an average price of say, twenty dollars a piece for a total of bazillions of dollars. (I don't know how much a bazillion is, but it's a lot!) For each product there were an average of forty paid professional musicians and engineers, not to mention huge staffs of artists, technicians, marketing strategists and promoters. Every television show, radio broadcast and movie produced enlisted the aid of well paid composers, arrangers, and performers to give life to their stories and pictures. In all, the professional music industry is a gazillion dollar business worldwide and shows no sign of slowing down, even when the rest of the economy is tenuous at best. The bottom line: music makes money!

This year on Capitol Hill it is a well known fact that the strongest lobbying organizations with the most effective results enlisted the help of high profile celebrities who gained their recognition and audience due to their involvement and success in the music industry including Paul Simon, Beverly Sills, Placido Domingo, and Bono. The bottom line: musicians dictate legislation that becomes law! Music rules!

And here's one I must include because I know it to be true. On April 29,1989 over fifteen thousand young people gathered in Washington D.C. to sing as part of a program called "America Sings." Through their efforts they were able to raise over $200,000 to help less fortunate peers reflected in the one hundred thousand homeless children in America. The impact of "America Sings" continues to grow, their influence continues to expand because the bottom line: music saves lives!

Now that we have our facts straight;I have a challenge to all of us as musicians who know for another fact that music can make kings stand up and walls fall down. Let's get off our *molto grande* insecurities, out of our annual cocktail parties and board room discussions and put to practical use our power as artists and educators. Let's use our collective creative genius to make a better world using music as our primary, formidable tool. Let's prove that we are not an extracurricular activity to be squeezed in between fifth and sixth period every other Thursday. We are the movers and the shakers and the doers. With all humility, the school, the church, the entire community centers on us! (Even if at times they are reluctant to admit it). Because of the universality of our art, we have broader influence in this world than any other group of people. We are essential! We give focus to kids lives. We are powerful! We raise consciousness and dollars. We are rich with influence! We set the tone of our society's nows and forevers. We are the difference! We save lives!

Finally, to my friend Tim who, "wants to sing," me too Tim, me too, for the grandest and simplest of reasons.

I want to sing for jubilation and despair,
for loss and gain, for anger and for teasing,
for pain and suffering, for frustration and exaltation,
for history and love and longing, for hungry and homeless,
helpless and hopeless, for kind and unkind, for awe and inspiration,
for learning and for teaching, for celebration and for mourning,
for ego and humility, for grief and for joy.

I want to sing Tim, because when I do, every day, everyone, everything IS different!

Because We Sing
With Mac Huff

Because we sing, the world shines brighter.
Because we sing, we take away all fear.
Let music ring and your heart beats lighter;
And love will live forever because we sing.

Listen to the language that speaks right to the heart.
Listen to the sound of life, giving love a start.
A song is in the air, a song is ev'rywhere.
Lift your voice in joy and sing!

Because we sing, the world shines brighter.
Because we sing, we take away all fear.
Let music ring and your heart beats lighter;
And love will live forever because we sing.

Music is a light growing deep inside of me,
Shining heart to heart it grows in perfect harmony.
Beating like the sun, a song for ev'ryone.
Lift your voice in joy and sing!

Because we sing of hope, our hearts implore,
Let music never cease beyond the stars our song will soar.
We dream a world of peace because we sing.

THE SHIP I SAIL

It occurred to me one day that I would never be an Olympian. It was sobering. I was in my mid-forties by the time I finally admitted it to myself, but I think most of us have this thing in the back of our minds that it might just happen … yet. You know, they might make show choir a new event or something. It's like (and I'm not kidding now) I have kinetic dreams. I mean sometimes in my dreams I can actually do some amazing athletic feats. One of them is to stand in the front yard and do a back flip. Isn't that weird? I know. But I'm not kidding! In my mind and in my body I can feel the feeling of doing a back flip even though in reality I would without a doubt land on my head and hurt the lawn. Still, I can feel it as though it's real.

Another kinetic dream I have is the feeling of diving off a diving board into a deep, clear blue swimming pool. It's not so much the dive that I dream of as the bounce on the end of the board. I swear to you, I can feel it in my legs and knees as though I was actually doing it. I stretch my arms; take a preparatory step and land with grace and beauty at the very edge of the board. It bends way down and catapults me high into the air where I suppose I go on to accomplish a perfect half gainer in a pike position, but my dream never gets that far.

Okay, and the last kinetic dream I have is the feeling of swinging a baseball bat and really connecting with the ball. No kidding! I stand at home plate wiggling my hips and glaring at the pitcher, my spikes gripping the sandy soil. The meatball comes and I smash that thing a country mile! Truly, truly I say unto you, "I can feel it!" In my dreams. Analyze that, baby!

Mac just sent me the final manuscript of a new song we've been working on called "The Ship I Sail." It's about the choices that come up in life and the hope that when the opportunity arises we make good decisions.

One of the best choices I ever made in my life (and believe me there's been some questionable ones) was to make music and the teaching of children the main focus of my professional life. It wasn't necessarily a conscious decision, although I guess I did choose music education as my major in college. But in truth it just happened to be the ship that was in the harbor the day I decided to board. It was a particular ship that for me has managed to sail true. It has been an unforgettable and rewarding voyage lasting more than twenty-five years.

At the time, I never really knew what journey this ship would take on its long voyage. What I did know was that in music there is a force that can move people to do extraordinary things. What I did know was that young people and music is a combination that can truly change the world. And what I did know was that it is the responsibility of adults to help guide these young people in the discovery of how to use the potential their youth, their energy and yes, their music provides them.

What I did know was that young people and music is a combination that can truly change the world.

There are a bazillion stars in the sky just as there are a bazillion inspirations in the minds of humankind. Helping young people decide which stars are worthy to follow is an assignment that teachers passionately embrace. I have often said that helping young people discover the song inside of them and encouraging them to sing it is one of the great roles we play as teachers and parents. But what I may not have stated clearly and yet, quite fervently believe is that not just any song will do. Singing a song that makes a positive contribution to the planet is the one to try to discover inside yourself and the one to share with the world.

There are voices of many calling out to all of us; some are filled with noble ideas, some are less so. Helping young people decide which voices to listen to is a worthy assignment that good teachers embrace.

Finally, there are many paths to pursue in life. There are paths that may lead to great fortune and little happiness. There are paths that serve your self and there are paths that serve others. There are opportunities to use your time, energy, and talent to make the world a better place for yourself or a better place for everyone. Helping young people decide which path to choose is a worthy assignment that good teachers heartily embrace.

More than twenty-five years ago my ship came in. It was filled with passengers I have grown to love and admire. By "passengers" I mean all of the literally tens of thousands of students and teachers who have made this journey called music education together. And we journey on. There are still students who need our help. There are still developing young singers who need our guidance. There is still a noble mission for us to approach together with each other and our music. It is a worthy assignment that teachers of any subject, and perhaps music most of all gladly embrace.

So, I guess I won't be an Olympian. Except in my kinetic dreams I may never do a perfect half gainer in a pike position into a pool of clear blue water. I may never hit a meatball out of the park or stand in the front yard and do a stylish back flip. But I do not sigh.

Long ago, being a teacher was the ship I chose to sail. It still is. To my fellow teachers I want to say that I am happy to be a sea with you remarkable people, because when all is sung and done, I like the wake we make.

The Ship I Sail

With Mac Huff

Lo, noble star among the heaven's lights,
Woe beyond my reach, but ne'er out of mortal sight,
Mine eyes are fast upon thy possibility
Let this be the single star I see.
Let this be the star I see.

O gallant voice quakes not in ocean's breeze,
Alas nearly lost in quivering human seas,
Calling men to honor and all to shy from fear,
Let this be the steady voice I hear.
Let this be the voice I hear.

Ah! Ship of lofty dreams and charity,
Sail forth in peace upon this wondrous sea.
Courage in your prow, in your wake, grace shall prevail.
Let this be the mighty ship I sail.

Let this be the voice,
Let this be the star,
Let this be the ship I sail.
Let this be the ship I sail.

So, dear friends, like a good Lutheran I'd like to end this all with a blessing to you and yours. I don't suppose I have any actual Irish blood in me that can be easily raced, but then again, are we all not just a little bit Irish? And English. German and French, Kenyan and Pakistani, Mexican and Chinese? In the end, it all runs happily together I believe; like honey, like space, ah indeed, like music.

A King's Irish Blessing

With Cristi Cary Miller

O gentle friends long ol' Upland stream
Were I king, oh what treasures I'd bare.
I, being poor, have only my dreams,
Shivering prayers I might spare.

May you all live as long as you think you might want
Never want as long as you live.
May the sunshine be bright on your dark window pane
And rainbows follow each rain
Oh rainbows will follow each rain.

Too rye lee oo rye lee ay
Too rye lee oo rye lee ay
Too rye lee oo rye lee ay
Too rye lee oo rye lee ay

May your purse be so heavy and your heart so light
May you live one hundred more years.
And may good luck pursue you each morning and night
May you feel more laughter than tears.

May the hills of your homeland forever caress you
As you sit with your friends by the fire.
May the luck of the Irish continue to bless you
And all that your heart may desire
Oh, all that your heart may desire.

O gentle friends long ol' Upland stream
I've no royal treasure, it's true
I, being poor, have only my dreams,
And a humble blessing for you.
Oh, this humble blessing for you.

ACKNOWLEDGMENTS